PAPERBARK
PUBLISHING

COPYRIGHT © 2024 WENDY C. WILSON
Published by Paperbark Publishing
All rights reserved. This book or parts thereof may not be reproduced in any form, stored in any retrieval system, or transmitted in any form by any means, electronic, mechanical, photocopy, recording, or otherwise, without prior written permission of the publisher, except as provided by United States of America copyright law. For information regarding permission requests, write to *wwilsonus@gmail.com*.

ISBN	eBook	979-8-9903684-0-8
	Paperback	979-8-9903684-1-5
	Hardcover	979-8-9903684-2-2

Library of Congress Control Number: 2024905537

First Edition
Book Production and Publishing by Brands Through Books
brandsthroughbooks.com

www.wendycwilson.com

IRON WILL

How to Heal Your Invisible Scars, Unlock Confidence, and Achieve the Freedom You've Always Wanted

WENDY C. WILSON

PAPERBARK
PUBLISHING

"A real and raw journey that everyone must read. Wendy has poured her heart and soul into letting us know that we can go from trauma to triumph. A must-read!"

—*Sheena Yap Chan*, *Wall Street Journal* best-selling author, keynote speaker, consultant, and creator of the award-winning podcast *The Tao of Self-Confidence*

"In *Iron Will*, Wendy C. Wilson bravely shares her inspiring journey of resilience and triumph over childhood trauma, domestic abuse, and workplace adversity. Her raw honesty, coupled with practical strategies for overcoming life's toughest challenges, makes this memoir a must-read for anyone seeking to harness their own inner strength. Wilson's story is a powerful reminder that no matter how dark the path may seem, there is always hope for a brighter future."

—*Ashley Mansour*, international best-selling author and award-winning producer and writer

*To my husband, Alan, and my children,
Samantha and Adrian.*

*This book is a testament to the love
and support you've given me.*

Contents

Introduction   1

Chapter 1.   Finding My Voice—   5
              A Journey to Empowerment
              and Purpose

Chapter 2.   A Childhood in Turmoil   13

Chapter 3.   The "Lucky" Few   19

Chapter 4.   Behind Closed Doors   29

Chapter 5.   Who Am I?   39

Chapter 6.   I Married My Father!   47

Chapter 7.   Alone but Free   61

Chapter 8.   The Escape   69

Chapter 9.   A New Chapter   89

Chapter 10.   I Am Not Ugly After All   101

Chapter 11.   Empowerment Through Adversity—   111
              The Iron Will Framework

Your Journey Doesn't End Here   141

Acknowledgments   143

About the Author   145

Endnotes   147

Introduction

IF I WERE TO ASK YOU to describe your childhood experience in one word, what would that word be for you? Mine is *fear*.

I lived in constant fear when growing up with my father, mother, father's mistress, and six other siblings under one roof. My father's regular beatings of my mom were the main source of that fear.

For more than fifty years, since I was about eight, I have had the same recurring nightmare. It is a dark and rainy night. Amid the heavy downpour, flashing lightning, and rolling thunder, I am leading my mother and my other siblings through a dense forest, headed for the car. We are running away from my father. My heart is pounding in my throat as I whisper urgently for everyone to hurry up. When I look back, I can see my mom tightly holding on to my little brother's hand, struggling to keep up with me and my sisters. The look of fear in their eyes mirrors the fear I feel in my heart. It seems to take forever for us to get to the car. Once there, I jump in, start the car, and drive away with everyone squeezed in the back and me squinting through drops of rain flowing down my face. I can feel my wet clothes sticking to me, the chill that runs down my spine, and goosebumps all down both my arms. I have had this nightmare regularly for over fifty years, and never once have I gotten past this stage of the nightmare. I will always jerk wide awake at this exact part, heart pounding and feeling the chill of the wet clothes as if they are still on me.

So . . . the question remains, subconsciously in my mind anyway, did I really get away? Also, why am I the one driving? I was eight when this dream started! In analyzing this dream now, I question, do I feel responsible for the safety of my family, or is this nightmare more of an expression of my guilt in not jumping in to help and this is my way of helping? For most of the beatings, I was hiding in fear! Then the questions start flooding into my mind again: Could I have done something? Would it have made a difference? Those are the questions that continue to swirl in my mind and haunt me after every one of these nightmares. This guilt has haunted me for a long time and is debilitating.

I cannot remember a time growing up when my father was with us that there was any laughter. For me, there was only fear. On the contrary, when he was not home, I felt unrestricted and free to express myself, laughing and playing. More on that later.

Fear paralyzed me throughout my childhood. Especially whenever my father was home, I felt like I was walking through a field with buried landmines, being very careful where I stepped so I would not cause my father to explode and beat my mom. I felt tense and was always looking out for the triggers that indicated he would be looking for any reason to fly into a rage. I spent my days trying to make sure no one was mad at me and suppressing my own opinions, feelings, and needs to accommodate others—sound familiar, people pleasers out there? My focus, unfortunately, was on getting approval from my family more than my own needs and desires. I also got to a point where I became very good at predicting and detecting my father's triggers. I am especially vigilant during the evening hours, on weekends, and on public holidays. I carried with me the guilt of not stepping in to stop the beatings. This guilt translated into feelings of worthlessness, low self-esteem, and a lack of confidence in myself. Additionally, keeping all the secrets—not letting any of our friends know of this physical abuse—locked inside of me was unhealthy for my mind, body, and soul.

Throughout this book, I will take you through my journey as a child witnessing my father physically abuse my mom; the physical and emotional abuse I experienced as an adult; the bullying and discrimination I endured in my corporate life; and how I wrestled with guilt, self-worthlessness, cripplingly low self-esteem, and a pervasive lack of confidence. My journey is a testament to overcoming these daunting obstacles and rediscovering my inner strength and sense of self. But this narrative isn't just mine to tell—it's also an invitation to you, the reader, to embark on your own journey of self-discovery and resilience. Throughout the pages of this book, I promise not only to share my story but also to offer you the tools and insights necessary for cultivating your own iron will.

When reading about the trauma of my childhood, it's important to note that my perspective is strictly based on my personal experiences. I understand others may have different perspectives on how they saw those events unfold. It's similar to when five people witness an accident and are asked to describe it; there will be five different versions of the story. Although I want to acknowledge and respect the fact that each of us may have our own unique recollections and interpretations, there is no denying that my father severely abused my mom for as long as he lived. By sharing my own story, I aim to create a narrative that is both honest and understanding of the diverse perspectives, even within my own family. It is my intention to approach this topic with sensitivity and focus only on my own journey.

We can't do anything about our past, but I believe we can start promoting healthier self-perceptions and emotional well-being today by taking some simple steps to help create a more inclusive and supportive environment for individuals, including children, dealing with self-esteem and labeling issues. Furthermore, children need to understand that true beauty and value are not defined by skin color or external appearances but by who we are as individuals.

Although I am an adult now and have lived apart from my parents for many years, the residual effects of living in such a toxic environment have remained with me. Publicly, I have been seen as a happy, well-adjusted individual, but I cannot shake this nagging in the back of my mind that I am not enough, that I am a fraud—*Wait till they find out who you really are!* It is as if the stains of my childhood and failure in my first marriage are tattooed on my heart, mind, and soul. No matter how much I try to ignore them or pretend they never happened, they stick with me.

CHAPTER 1

Finding My Voice—
A Journey to Empowerment
and Purpose

AFTER OVER THIRTY-FIVE YEARS in corporate America, my husband and I had the opportunity to move three hours away from our home of fifteen years in Chicago, Illinois, to Madison, Wisconsin. I decided it was time for me to leave the corporate world. I felt this move would provide me with a chance to slow down, get a taste of what retirement is all about, and maybe even take time to smell the proverbial roses! I knew I would need to have something to continue to mentally challenge myself. I've read that, statistically, those who had been going at 120 mph for many years and suddenly stopped or radically slowed down all activities when they retired died within two years of their retirement. I don't want to be one of those statistics. Excitedly, since it would take me several more months to wind things down at work, I scheduled time on the weekends to figure out what I wanted to do in the next phase of my life outside of corporate.

After a couple of weekends, I came up with a big blank page. Zip. Zero. *Who Am I? What do I like to do?* It was depressing, to say the least. I realized that between juggling my busy sixty- to seventy-hour workweek for over thirty-five years, keeping up with the kids' activities (homework and extracurricular activities), and managing the household, I didn't really know who I was anymore! I had lost my identity as a person outside of my career! I had no problem with who I was professionally, since I got a lot of my self-worth from my achievements at work. It is less messy that way; work responsibilities are predictable and controllable (to a certain extent, anyway). I could easily and quickly rattle off who I was and what I did at work. You can see I was in a sorry state! On the personal side of my life, the children and husband always came first. What do they want to do, what do they like to eat, where do they want to go for vacation, and so on and so forth. It didn't help that I am a big people pleaser on this nonprofessional side of the fence. It is always about what others—family, friends, even neighbors—want. I have difficulty saying "no" or setting boundaries for fear of disappointing others. I'm constantly seeking approval or validation from others and experiencing guilt or anxiety when I don't consider others' needs first.

I felt extremely sad. And as always, I brushed that aside and got to work. I knew I could figure this out. My initial strategy was to start journaling. I thought maybe I would find my identity through journaling, or at least gain enough of a sense of who I am and what I like to do for me to move forward with my planning. To my surprise, I found journaling very therapeutic. Instead of journaling on what I wanted to do next, I was drawn to just writing out my feelings, which led me to write about my past. The more I journaled, the easier it got to express myself, and everything just started to flow out of me. The emotional lock that I had unconsciously placed on my heart was busted open by the simple act of writing!

I think it was especially freeing to finally be able to let out all that fear and sadness that had been locked in me for so many years. Letting the tears and words flow out of me wasn't easy emotionally, but the more I journaled, the lighter I felt. I also felt safe since it was on paper and no one would know unless I let them read it. What journaling also revealed to me was that I have not just lived through but survived a very traumatic childhood and an adult life fraught with physical and emotional abuse while being ostracized, marginalized, discriminated against, and discounted at work. I saw what had helped me in the darkest moments and how I was able to persevere through my situations. Bingo, a light bulb turned on in my head. I could help others do the same by sharing my stories and, more importantly, how I overcame these traumas—*I found my purpose for this next phase of my life!*

In those early days when I was in the midst of tremendous pain and going through the darkest moments of my life, I often cried out to God, asking Him about the purpose for my suffering. I knew then that there *had* to be a purpose. It took me a few decades to get here. Now, I understand. After decades, I have my answer. Thank you! My pain was not for naught. Without enduring and overcoming these challenges, I would not have gained the experience and knowledge necessary to guide others who've had similar struggles. Now I can offer hope and strategies, helping them to discover their own strengths; break through the chains that are holding them back; reclaim their lives; and come out the other side a strong, joyful, and fulfilled individual. Hence this book you are holding in your hands.

I also started a blog (www.wendycwilson.com) on how to navigate corporate challenges in the workplace. Those work-life challenges can be equally debilitating.

Before I continue, I would like to emphasize that I am not a psychiatrist, psychologist, counselor, or any type of mental health care professional. The content of this book is based solely on my personal experience and perspective. While I have made efforts to provide accurate and helpful information, it is important to consult with a qualified mental health professional or therapist for personalized advice and support. This book is intended to share my own journey and insights and should not be considered a substitute for professional guidance. Please seek professional help if you are in need of mental health support.

My father was a functional alcoholic and a mean drunk. His excuse for drinking? It was all his father's fault. He hated his father for "abandoning" his mother and having a second wife, then a third, and then a fourth. My grandfather was a highly educated general in the army in China who spoke Mandarin, English, and Japanese fluently. During his time, the perception of a man's wealth was tied to how many wives one had. The wealthier one was, the more wives and households he could afford to support. In my opinion, at least my grandfather was more humane for keeping all four of his wives in separate households.

When my grandfather decided to relocate to Hong Kong, he left his wives and sent my father (his heir to the family name) to Malaysia to connect and live with a friend there. My father was only seventeen at the time. Years later, when he deemed he was in a better financial situation, my grandfather sent for his second wife and children to join him in Hong Kong, leaving his first wife (my father's mother) behind. My father would send money home regularly to help support his mother and her servants. I am sure wives number three and four did not stick around too long after he left since we never heard anything about them, except that the fourth wife was Japanese. In later years, my father's half brother and his daughter reached out to connect with us. My older sisters were in communication with our uncle and cousin and stayed in touch over the years. My father encouraged me to write to my grandfather when I was little, and I was delighted when he wrote back. In subsequent letters, he told me about his garment factory in Hong Kong. This didn't last, as I could only write when my father allowed. We were so accustomed to only obeying what my father asked of us that when he didn't ask me to continue to write to my grandfather, I didn't dare ask for permission to do so. My grandparents passed away when I was in my teens, and with that went the opportunity for me to reconnect with my grandfather as an adult.

My father was not just a drunk, he was also a womanizer. I guess the apple didn't fall far from the tree after all—at least the womanizer part, because my grandpa never smoked, drank, or physically abused his wives. My father, on the other hand, frequented bars, getting drunk and into fights wherever he went. He was the young and handsome "foreigner" that was the talk of the small town in Penang, Malaysia, and lived it up with a gang of equally brash, disruptive, and rowdy friends.

My mother, Pauline, had to quit school in second grade, as her mother could only afford to send one child to school. Naturally, the son (her younger brother) was the one who was sent to school. My maternal grandfather left his wife and three children with no support. They struggled, having no education or skills. My grandmother would do domestic chores for others—washing clothes, cooking, and the like—to supplement her income from her business running a small apothecary.

Many folks went to her for her natural homemade remedies to cure common illnesses. She was known to be highly intuitive. My mother and some of us inherited that trait. My mother and her older sister also helped out. My mom was a beautiful and vivacious young woman, known as the "beauty of Penang" at that time. When my father heard this, he made a bet with his gang of friends that he would be able to "get" this eighteen-year-old beauty of Penang, and he won that bet.

Within a year of being married to my mom, my father met Mona, a dance hostess, at one of the bars he frequented and fell in love with her. Shortly after, Mona became his full-time mistress. What my father hated his father for doing, abandoning his mother, he turned around and did to my mom. But wait . . . according to him, he did not abandon his wife; he just made his wife live under the same roof as his mistress! In his mind, he was not like his father at all. He provided for his wife, children (all seven of us), and his mistress. He prided himself on not "abandoning" his wife. To this day, I cannot see why that would be something to be proud of. In my opinion, 90 percent of the problems in our family stemmed from this very living arrangement—two women, sharing one husband, living in the same house. The fights were primarily about sex. It was simply cruel! Not just to my mom, but to Mona as well.

My mom was pregnant with her second child at that time. She had no say in the matter, and any opposition would have been met with severe beatings, which at the time were only occasional. Since my mom only had a second-grade education and no means to support herself or her children, she was totally dependent on her husband, and there was nowhere she could go. In her mind, she was stuck with her husband and had to accept the living arrangements that he dictated.

Before I was born, life became harder and harder for our family in Malaysia as the number of mouths to feed increased. Not long after my mom gave birth to her third daughter, my father up and moved the family, including Mona, to Hong Kong, and then to Singapore a few years after, in search of better employment opportunities. In Hong Kong, my mother had three more daughters. I consider it a blessing that Mona was unable to have children. I cannot even begin to imagine what life would have been like for all of us if she were to have had children of her own. Would my mom have had even more beatings for supposedly favoring her own children? There could have been a multitude of additional issues, but they, thankfully, did not materialize because Mona did not have her own children. Times were really hard then, so much so that there was no money for any of the powdered milk that we all grew up with. Fresh milk was imported and, therefore, only for the rich. Mom had to dissolve sugar in water in place of milk for the two youngest daughters, who were not yet on solid foods.

My mom told me that when my fifth sister got very sick, throwing up and running an extremely high temperature, she stood in line at the free clinic waiting all day for my sister to be seen by a doctor. At that time, free clinics in Singapore played a critical role in providing health care services for the less privileged segments of the population. They were usually run by a mix of charitable organizations, religious groups, and sometimes the colonial government or local municipal authorities. Due to the high demand for services at these free clinics, staff and volunteer shortages often affected the quality of service and efficiency of attendance to the sick. After a whole day of waiting, my mom was told again she had to wait her turn. Out of sheer desperation, she pushed her way to the front and pleaded with the nurses for a doctor to take a look at her child. The nurse took one look at my sister and knew she was in very bad shape. They immediately took her in and got a doctor to attend to her. Unfortunately, it was too late. My sister's high fever and vomiting had dehydrated her very badly; sitting in a facility with no air conditioning in hot and humid, tropical, eighty-five-degree weather didn't help either. She passed away. I know this affected my father deeply. According to the Chinese Lunar Calendar, my sister was born in the Year of the Rabbit. As long as I can remember, we were never allowed to have any pictures or toys of rabbits. We were not even allowed to draw or talk about rabbits as long as we were in my father's house. He didn't want to be reminded of his failure to provide for her. I can only imagine my parents' pain when they lost their child, my sister.

Four years later, I was born. And I lived in terror of my father from the moment I became a toddler. That was the age I could grasp what anger was and see the resulting consequences of my father's, even though I was not fully able to understand why he held so much of it.

CHAPTER 2

A Childhood in Turmoil

IN SINGAPORE, MY FATHER continued to struggle to put food on the table. The more he struggled, the more he took his frustrations out on my mother, about two to three times a month by then. Sometimes nothing provoked such beatings. When I got older, my mom told me it could be as mundane as when he came home from work and saw Mona had been crying. Without asking why she was upset, he would drag my mother by her hair into one of the bedrooms and start beating her up. During one severe beating, Mona shouted that she was crying because of her menstrual pain and that my mom had nothing to do with it. Looking back now, I can see why he did it—he wanted to send a clear message to my mom to behave and be very, very careful how she treated Mona, even when he was not around. Doesn't make it right, but that was how controlling he could be.

On one other such occasion, my father had my mom pinned down by kneeling on her chest, pummeling her face and attempting to strangle her. In desperation to breathe, my mom told me she grabbed his "jewels" and squeezed them. In the blinding pain, he snapped and almost killed her. At that time, I was only a toddler and can not remember the details, but I do remember the terror. We lived in two rooms of a huge rambling multi-tenant house owned by an old woman. This eighty-year-old landlady came into the room and knelt down, begging my father to stop. Whether he was moved by the old lady and couldn't take the burden of having an older person beg him or couldn't take the pain of his balls being squeezed, he finally let go and left the house. My mother's injuries were severe, but she couldn't afford to go to a hospital, not to mention that doing so might have caused my father to lose face or, worse, face arrest for attempting to kill his wife. She applied some topical medication and took lots of painkillers. It took a very long time for her to heal. The worst of the injuries was to her sternum area; my mother was a small woman, and my father's weight on her chest for a prolonged time had probably caused some severe internal injuries. For the rest of her life, the discomfort there continued to bother her.

So . . . Who Else Got Beaten in This Household?

Two of the six girls got most of the beatings from my father when we were growing up. Was it a conscious choice which child to beat?

From my mother's standpoint, I think not. She caned us (using small bamboo and sometimes rattan cane) when we disobeyed her. Corporal disciplinary punishment of children by their parents is not illegal in Singapore, although it is not encouraged by the government. This practice of light caning as punishment was introduced during the period of British colonial rule in Singapore. The common belief in those days was that to spare the rod was to spoil the child, which was derived from a verse in the Bible.[1] Small, fresh slash scars on legs caused by these light cane strikes were common among our schoolmates. I got minimal caning from my mom. As much as I would like to think I was such a good kid, the truth is I would just stand there for Mom to exact her punishment. How long can you punish a child who just stands there and takes it? Meanwhile, my older sisters would run, causing her to chase them down. The more she had to chase, the angrier she got and the harder and longer they were caned when caught. As we got older, my siblings grumbled that I was "special." I don't think I was; I was just a little quicker in figuring out how to get by with as little caning as possible!

For my father, I believe it was a choice. He chose who he would take his anger out on versus who he would spare. When there were just three girls, the oldest was the one who was constantly beaten. That was because the other two were more bothersome, and it would be just as well to not have to deal with them.

When the family grew to seven kids, my father continued his regular beatings of Mother, but Terri, the middle child, became an additional target for him. Terri was taller and stronger than the rest of us at that time, so my father probably thought she could take his beatings. Mona also jumped on the bandwagon to beat this sister once in a while since she was the "middle child" and no one's obvious favorite. These beatings from my father were not like the light discipline that my mother exacted on us occasionally; they were severe beatings. I remember one especially brutal beating of Terri by my father. He beat her so hard, and for so long, her flesh split open in several places on her legs and thighs. He did it because he was especially angry with her for crying for too long! He continued to beat her, telling her he would not stop until she stopped crying. Traumatic for a child? You bet. In addition, Terri told me she was teased and laughed at by her schoolmates for going to school with so many of those obviously deep, fresh scars—something she never forgot. Today, someone would have called Child Protective Services for sure. It was child abuse!

During another one of the bad beatings, Terri decided not to cry, remembering she was so severely beaten because she cried for too long the last time. She gritted her teeth and refused to cry out. Yep, you guessed it—he would not stop beating her until she cried out in pain! He got more and more mad as not a sound came from her. So, he beat her harder and harder and said he was going to "beat the stubbornness out of her." You are damned if you do and damned if you don't: confusing messages for a child! The biggest cruelty, I believe, was apparent in this instance. He was beating her because he was furious that his valuable antique vase was broken. My brother had accidentally broken it while roughhousing with Terri. Because the son was too precious to beat, he made the choice and picked this daughter to vent his anger on. Fair? Not from a rational person's perspective.

This time, even he thought he had gone too far. That night after the beating, he asked my mother to go and buy some crushed pearl powder, mixed it in water, and had my sister drink it. It was believed at the time that pearl powder could heal internal injuries, and it was also used to alleviate pain. Many years later, when we were all older adults, for the fun of it, we went to a Chinese physician who was supposedly known for healing any aches, pains, and internal injuries we have in our bodies using Chi (internal energy). We found the concept fascinating and decided to try it out while I was back in Singapore for a visit. After he treated this sister, he asked her if she had had a severe accident when she was young. He told her he could feel when treating her that she had some deep, old internal injuries. The day after this treatment, her back was covered with black and blue bruises because this Chinese physician's treatment had apparently released those old internal injuries to the surface of her skin. My father's severe beating of her when she was young came straight to her mind!

Another victim was the family dog. I don't remember what prompted this beating of the dog, but to this day I can still hear her howling in pain as my father pummeled her. The next day, he went out and bought a durian (a fruit and very expensive local delicacy) and gave it to the dog. I am not a psychologist, but was he feeling guilty for almost killing the dog? For years after this incident, when he was sitting in the kitchen, the dog would not walk past him but would make a wide circle to get around him. From my experience owning dogs, they are very forgiving; not a minute after you scold them for their bad behavior, they will love on you. The beatings must have been so severe and traumatic that our dog never forgot!

During one of his drunken episodes at an outdoor café in his younger days, much to the amusement of his drunken friends, he grabbed ahold of a stray cat by its tail and swung it around and around, hitting its head on the concrete floor until the cat died. It was all because the cat was "irritating" him by coming around and begging for scraps! It should have been a clear warning to my mom that there was a violent side to the man she was dating when this incident occurred. Hindsight is 20/20, as they say; she was eighteen and head over heels in love!

As mentioned earlier, my father chose not to take his anger out on our brother and punished Terri instead. Another child he chose to spare is me.

I hate my father!

CHAPTER 3

The "Lucky" Few

MY FATHER BELIEVED THAT I was the "lucky" child who brought him his son. My mom had seven daughters and one son. Mom was not allowed to stop till she bore a son, an heir to the family name, because Mona was never able to have any children. I am daughter number seven, who brought the number eight child, a son. Also, according to a little red book (some kind of almanac he consulted regularly to know when it was auspicious to do or not do certain things), I was born at a certain time, day, and year that made me the one who would bring luck to him. True to his belief, he saw his financial situation improve after I was born, which eventually enabled him to buy a four-bedroom house for us. Superstitions aside, I believe that when he thought he had a child who would bring him luck and prosperity, his focus on that belief was what caused him to do better financially. That is to say that whatever we consistently focus on becomes our reality. It had nothing to do with me. I was "lucky" only in the sense that he thought so.

An irony I observed back then was that my father named this house "Tranquilla," which stands for peaceful, quiet, and tranquil. He even had a beautiful bronze plate made with the name on it that hung at the gate. What happened within the four walls of this house was anything but tranquil!

We lived in a small neighborhood among expatriates from the British Royal Navy and their families. Initially, we were one of the only two Asian families in this neighborhood and had the most wonderful neighbors. When my sisters were at school and my father at work, Mom would allow my brother and me to go outside to play. Sometimes we would just explore in our own small yard, hunting for snails and slugs. Yep, I was a sweaty, rough-and-tumble little girl growing up. I preferred climbing trees over playing with dolls. Maybe it was because we never had dolls growing up.

Other times, we hung out with the neighborhood kids, chasing butterflies and trying to catch caterpillars and all kinds of insects. My brother and I were close then, and although he is younger, he was very protective of me, always taking my side when arguments broke out between my sisters and me. I, on the other hand, exerted my dominance over him. You see, he got the toys, and I didn't. So, if he wanted me to play with him, I would demand to be the main character of any story we were acting out. For example, I must be Robin Hood so I got to hold the bow and arrow. Or I had to be the hero knight so I got to wear the Roman helmet my parents bought him. Sometimes, when my mother took him with her on her shopping trips and bought him candy, he would ask her if he could have two so he could bring me one. How do I know this? When I refused to share my goodies with my brother, my mom would chide me, saying, "Your brother is always thinking of you when I buy him candy." I remember those days fondly, and those memories are like a few shiny spots in a very dark and scary world.

It goes to show that when we look for it, even in the darkest of times, we can find a spark of light, no matter how fleeting, and no matter how faint. As a child, I lived for those fun moments with my brother when everything was bright and the sky always seemed to be blue and filled with fluffy cumulus clouds. Not to mention, I got to be in charge!

Am I indeed lucky that my father chose not to beat me? I don't feel in the least bit lucky or blessed or special. On the contrary, I feel guilty for not sharing in the burden of being beaten like my other siblings and mother were. Perhaps if I was also beaten, there would have been fewer beatings for them. I know now that is irrational thinking. I was not in control of those circumstances, but that doesn't make me feel less responsible for not trying to help stop the beatings. I have carried that burden with me for years. Punishments, even if directed at one person, often involve all.

When one of my older sisters was in middle school, Youth for Christ International was very actively spreading its message in schools. She became a Christian through this group. My mother was beside herself trying to cover for her, thinking my father would surely kill her when he found out. My parents were Taoists, and we observed every ritual that came with it. Taoism, also known as Daoism, is an ancient Chinese philosophy and spiritual tradition that emphasizes living in harmony with the Tao (the Way or the Path), or the fundamental nature of the universe. Central to Taoist thought is the concept of wu wei, which advocates for effortless action and going with the natural flow of life. Taoists value simplicity, spontaneity, and tranquility, seeing these qualities as means to align with the Tao and achieve spiritual enlightenment.

We had an altar with a white statue of Confucius as a scholar. This altar sat front and center in our main living room. My father lit incense and candles at the altar during his daily morning and evening worship rituals. During prominent festivals and birthdays, all foods must first be offered to the idol before we humans can consume them. Although we didn't celebrate birthdays, when it was one of our birthdays, my mom would dye the shells of about a half dozen hard-boiled eggs red and offer them to the idol, asking him to bless the birthday girl or boy.

My sister, having become a Christian, would refuse to eat foods that were first offered to the idol, so my mom secretly put aside some food and hid it so she would have something to eat. When my sister started going to church on Sundays, my mom came up with a plan. My sister would take me and another sister with her so that if my father asked where we went, the story would be that she had taken us shopping. A mother's love for her children knows no bounds, especially when it comes to protecting them.

I loved those Sundays! My sister would drop us off at Sunday school—my first introduction to the Christian faith—while she attended the Sunday service. I enjoyed listening to the stories and, of course, the small bag of candy we got to take home at the end of class. I always finished them on the bus ride home from church, not saving any to share with my brother. My rationale was that he would not be able to keep the secret of where the candy came from. As always, I had to keep our trips to church a secret. It was easy for me since I was always in my own world daydreaming and didn't often talk to anyone, anyway.

This went on for a while, but eventually my sister started talking more openly about her beliefs, especially when my father was within earshot. We didn't talk *to* our father—all communications went through our mom. I suspect this was my sister's way of letting him know. She was a strong and independent girl who knew what she wanted. Since he was made aware of her going to church on Sundays, she stopped with the pretext of taking us shopping. I missed the candies and the stories. I also loved to go, as people there were always kind to me. I could relax when I was there.

This positive early exposure to Christianity never left me. As an adult, this same sister shared the salvation message with me when we had lunch together on a bright sunny afternoon. I accepted Jesus Christ as my Savior—one of the best decisions of my life. Although I am a Christian and will, from time to time, relate here how my faith has helped me, this is not a book about Christianity. I respect all religious beliefs and am convinced that no matter what your belief system is, when you reach out and connect with that source (whatever that higher power is to you), it will give you a sense of peace in the times when you need that comfort most. I believe we all need something to anchor us.

Since I was not going to church anymore, I was home for an event on a particular Sunday. While my sister was at church, Father calmly told us to go get the bricks that lined our side yard and throw them into her bedroom. This was a very different experience for me, as my father was not in a rage. He seemed calm, but I knew what he was asking us to do was because he was angry and punishing someone for it. There were two bunk beds in this small room, where four of my sisters slept. We were supposed to put the bricks in the middle of the room between the two bunk beds. At first, we would gently put the bricks down, but he demanded that we use maximum force to throw them into the middle of the room. In fact, he instructed us to stand at this bedroom's doorway and throw the bricks from there to the center of the room. This was to ensure maximum impact when the bricks hit the floor or each other. He sat on a chair along the pathway, watching us walk in and out carrying and throwing brick after brick. As I walked to and from the room, I dared not look at my father, and my heart pounded in my throat the whole time. I was terrified, anticipating that he would explode and start beating someone. After what seemed like several hours of this, we had a four-foot-high pile of bricks with dust everywhere. To this day, I don't know or even understand the point of this and doubt my other siblings did either, but no one dared ask! This pile of bricks stayed in the bedroom for several months. Although I didn't sleep in this bedroom, my clothes were in the closet there. I do remember having to pick my way carefully around this pile of bricks in the middle of the bedroom to get to the closet to get my clothes for school every day. I don't remember having to remove the bricks from the bedroom, though. My mom must have done it while we were at school.

I believe this was supposed to punish my sister for going to church, but we were the ones who had to do it. The irony of this is that my sister does not even remember this incident and has probably blocked it all out of her memory! Yet, I clearly remember the fear of those several hours, having to walk past my father and throw brick after brick into that bedroom with the dust from the broken bricks flying everywhere. So, who was he actually punishing?

As time passed, he started reading the Bible himself. In fact, I was told he read it from cover to cover two or three times. I suspect he was trying to understand what my sister was getting into, and I assume he relaxed his stance on her going to church because he saw it was not some kind of dangerous cult.

Then there were the times when he would ask my mom to lock the gate after a certain time so my sister would not be able to get back into the house after either her evening church events or when she was out on a date. Mom would lock the gate, but when he went to bed, she would sneak out and unlock it. I don't believe my sister ever knew this was going on as well; so, the ones whom my father was actually punishing were us, watching this from the sidelines!

The stressful part was not knowing what one could say or do at any time that would cause my father to fly into a rage. A couple of incidents stick in my memory to this day because they started out so innocently and trivially that his reactions to them, now that I look back at them, seem unusually harsh. It was like a child throwing tantrums to get attention. He was no child, but an adult who had incited so much fear in his family that he just did whatever he wanted because he knew he could. No one dared to step up to stop such unreasonably bad behavior.

First, my mom missed an ingredient in a dish my father had asked her to cook. At the dinner table, he pointed out that she had missed it, and she casually said, "It's okay because it is not one of the main ingredients of the dish." No matter how casually her response was made, it would be considered arguing or talking back to him. He flew into a rage, and the night ended with another round of beatings for my mother. The words my father said then stuck with me for the rest of my life: "If you don't want to do it right, don't do it!" This would not be the only or the first of such episodes.

I repeatedly heard this phrase from my father. I believe my perfectionistic tendencies came from this mantra that I had subconsciously seared into my mind. I am what I like to call a "recovering perfectionist" today, still working through letting it go. Unfortunately, I have worn this perfectionist tag as a badge of honor for so long, and derived so much satisfaction from being "perfect," it is hard to let go of. I am not perfect—no one is, by the way.

An approach I have found helpful is to reframe in my mind what *perfect* is. Many use the phrase "Done is better than perfect." But that does not work for me. Instead, I use an alternative phrase: "It will never be perfect, but this is the best I can do for now, so let it go." With that in mind, I send out the email, submit the report, mark the task complete, and move on to the next thing. We will review this in more detail later in the book. It took me a while to come up with my own phrase that worked for me. We are all unique, and no one way will work for everyone. Try out different ways. Most importantly, don't give up. Believe you will get there, and, with enough practice, you will!

Another form of punishment that I remember, and this one was for all of us in the family, was not being allowed to use cups or glasses to drink liquids. I don't know exactly what was said that caused my father to forbid us from using cups and glasses. This one lasted a long time. At first, we kids found it fun to use bowls to drink and didn't mind it at all. As time wore on, however, it started to be bothersome, at least for me. Thinking back to that time, the saddest part of this is that he was not home most of the day, and yet he had instilled so much fear in all of us that we did not even think of ignoring the order, even when he was not home. The fear of what he would do to those who disobeyed his orders was real!

As we navigated our father's unpredictable tirades as best we could, we understood one unspoken rule: the echoes of our cries and fear *must* be swallowed by the walls that bore witness to this silent pact—what happens in the family stays in the family.

CHAPTER 4

Behind Closed Doors

IT IS ALMOST AN UNSPOKEN RULE—we do not air our dirty laundry in public, causing our parents to lose face. I think this may be more common in Asian families. Have you ever seen an Asian family on *The Jerry Springer Show*? I haven't! *The Jerry Springer Show* was a long-running daytime tabloid talk show loaded with profanity and guests who were not afraid to embarrass themselves on national television over incest, adultery, and a host of other things people think of as dirty family laundry. To this day, my siblings and I have never shared our experiences of growing up with anyone, except maybe with our respective spouses. We don't even discuss them among ourselves. We all dealt with this childhood trauma in different ways. One never really gets over such traumas, but we can definitely learn to deal with them in healthy ways. It took me a long time. I often wonder if I would have found peace earlier in my life if I was able to talk it out and process my feelings with my siblings.

Although my siblings and I have not discussed any of this among us, I am grateful that my mom at least trusted me enough to confide in me. We never got into long discussions about anything she told me. There were times when I think she needed someone to just listen, and I am happy I was there. I believe she could open up to me because I just listened and empathized with her instead of rebuking or judging her. I will forever be grateful that I was given that opportunity, and I get a little peace knowing I was there for her, at least some of the time.

Like us, especially when we were younger, my mom was not allowed to have friends. She had a good friend in Singapore, who lived not too far away from us. My mom would occasionally take a detour after picking me up from school, and we would go visit her. They would sit down with cups of coffee at her kitchen table and catch up for an hour or so, laughing and having a grand time. Of course, I was sworn to secrecy about these visits. Another secret to keep.

My siblings and I had friends we interacted with during school hours but not outside of school. Since we didn't celebrate birthdays, there was no excuse for friends to come over, and we were not allowed to go over to friends' houses, much less stay overnight! There were no opportunities to hang out after school since my mother dropped us off and was always there waiting to take us home when we got out.

Birthdays generally passed by without any mention. For years, my parents were struggling to put food on the table, and celebrating birthdays was the furthest thing from their minds. Not much happened except for the red-dyed eggs, and sometimes my mom would cook a plate of noodles for us to share. Noodles are a symbol of long life—so auspicious to have them on birthdays. One year, my father gave me a "birthday present." I remember this occasion as clearly as if it had happened yesterday. My father came home, and as soon as he walked in the door and saw the plate of red-dyed eggs on the altar, he asked my mom whose birthday it was that day. I was right there next to him when Mom told him it was my birthday. He reached into his pocket, fished out a small bag of speckled Cadbury Creme Eggs, and handed it to me. I was over the moon! If I could've done a backflip, I would have done several right then. It didn't matter to me that it was only half a bag or that he didn't actually remember it was my birthday. It was my first and only birthday present from my father, ever. I was eight years old.

As we grew up, my father's rules on us having friends over relaxed. We still didn't have anyone come over often, but my older sisters were allowed to go out with friends after school and even have some occasionally stop by when my father was at work. I figured he knew there was no way he could continue to control us. Additionally, some of my sisters are much older than me, so they were already in their late teens or going either into college or out into the working world when I was still in elementary school. When those rules were relaxed for them, we, the younger ones, benefited from them. My father was also getting older and perhaps a little more mellow.

Those were the unspoken rules. There were also rules we had to live by. One of the major ones I remember was that we were not allowed to sleep past 7 a.m. On the rare occasions that we did, my father would turn the volume of his stereo so high that the small house would vibrate from the noise. A way to wake up, for sure! The reason for the rule? He said, "Only whores sleep late." He would know! I suppose this rule was for our own good; he didn't want his daughters to take up that profession. Fortunately for me, I have always been an early bird.

One Saturday morning, I walked into the kitchen and, not seeing my father there, I asked my mom, "Is Father awake yet?" Since his bedroom was right next to the kitchen, he overheard it as me asking, "Is Father dead yet?" In the Hokkien dialect, the words *awake* and *die* sound similar. Oh my, that's the worst thing a highly superstitious person can hear first thing in the morning! I was told later that day to never ever ask that question again. There are advantages to being the "lucky one" after all. *If asking that question would make it so, hmmm . . . maybe I ought to try it again sometime soon*, thought my young, rebellious self.

Dinnertime, when my father was home, was sacred. The table was laid out with all the proper settings for whether we were dining in the traditional Chinese way (using chopsticks and spoons) or in the Western style (using forks, knives, and spoons). We could only start when everyone was in their proper place. The three adults carried on the conversation, with my older sisters chiming in when questions were directed at them. One particular evening, when I was seven or eight, while polite dinner conversations were going on, my brother and I were having our own fun on the side. We were giggling and having a good time when my father stopped all conversations and banished my brother and me to under the table. There we stayed until dinner was over, and we were then sent directly to bed. It was meant to be a punishment, but my brother and I carried on nonverbally enjoying ourselves; in fact, I thought we had even more fun sitting under the dinner table in the company of everyone's legs!

Unfortunately, this was not so on another occasion. This time, except for our father, who was in his sitting room reading, we were all watching television after dinner. It must have been a comedy because we were all having a great time laughing out loud. In the middle of our laughter, my father walked out to the living room and turned off the television. Silence. No one moved. He turned without a word and left the room. We all got up and went quietly into our bedrooms. No one dared to ask, "Why did you turn off the TV?" We knew we were either too loud or maybe even having too much fun when he was in a bad mood and didn't want to hear laughter. Asking was not even a thought that would enter our young minds at that time. My mom, unless she wanted to get a slap, didn't say a word either. From then on, we laughed silently and sometimes had to clasp our hands tightly against our mouths to stifle any noise when our father was home.

My father's favorite place in the house was his sitting area. This was a small area off the hallway leading to the kitchen. There he had his stereo with gigantic speakers that seemed to fill up half the room (the technology of those early days) and his precious collection of Waterford crystal decanters with matching glasses for his liquor. Most of the time, he sat there to read. If I saw him in there with the lights turned down low and his classical music playing in the background (Chopin, Mozart, and Tchaikovsky were his favorites), I knew he was depressed about something and would be looking for any excuse to turn violent. Sometimes I thought he was psyching himself into that violent state of mind. Other times, I could tell he was already angry about something. Whether it was something someone said or did, he would sit in his chair in this room and start drinking, regardless of the time of day. The sound of ice cubes clinking against the side of a drinking glass and the smell of hard liquor still send chills of fear down my spine!

This was not something we discussed among us, but we would all intuitively sense the mood, and the house would become somber. Everyone would speak in whispers, and we would stay in our rooms. Holidays were especially vulnerable times since my father was home all day and the likelihood of him getting mad at something was higher—more opportunities for him to find fault with what someone said or did or didn't do.

Whenever my father was home during the day on the weekends, and he was not in a depressed mood, he was usually busy instructing my mother and all of us kids on what he wanted done and how to do it. Like one of my sisters used to say, "His hobby is our chore." Take, for example, one period of his life when he was interested in cultivating orchids. So, we had to help break up whole bricks and charcoal into smaller chunks so he could use them to plant his orchids. He did everything in extremes—it was not just a few pots of orchids, it was one hundred or more!

He enjoyed coming up with ways to cook different dishes that he had eaten during the week with colleagues so we could try them at home. Taking us all out to a restaurant would be way too expensive. He also took those opportunities to teach us how to eat certain foods. Take, for example, the artichoke. I learned how to eat a whole artichoke from him. My mom would steam and serve each one on a plate to us. Father taught us to peel each petal, dip it in the sauce, and use our teeth to gently squeeze out the tiny bit of flesh at the tip. After we finished nibbling the tiny morsels of the artichoke flesh from each petal, we could dig into the heart of the artichoke with our forks and knives. This was where the prize was after working diligently on each petal. My father didn't cook but would instruct my mother on how to do it.

Then there was the time when he was into keeping birds.

Each colorful songbird had its own ornate cage that needed to be cleaned regularly. On weekends, my father would send us younger children out to the fields to catch grasshoppers so they could be fed to his birds. We would spend hours in the hot sun beating the bushes and catching those critters. Next came fishes—from the exotic discus to the lionhead goldfish and the more common guppies. He had them all at one point or another. Once, my mom was overenthusiastic and cleaned out the home of all his precious lionhead goldfish, not knowing that she must allow the water to oxygenate before relocating the goldfish back to the clean water. Within a short period of time, all the goldfish were dead, floating with their big bellies up. Surprisingly, and much to my mom's relief, there were no beatings.

When he got quiet and stopped ordering everyone around, it was another one of those signs where I knew something was brewing beneath the surface and the storm was coming. Sometimes, the beatings came; other times, they didn't. The stress and anxiety of waiting for the other shoe to drop, so to speak, cannot be good for one's physical or mental health. I often joke that having lived in an environment like this, my heart has been stressed enough that it is most unlikely that I would suffer a heart attack from shock or stress!

I jest, but on a serious note, living in this perpetual state of fight-or-flight, also known as chronic stress, has profound effects on both the body and the psyche. Chronic activation of the body's stress response system, involving the hypothalamic-pituitary-adrenal axis and the sympathetic nervous system, can lead to a multitude of health issues, such as psychological, physiological, and behavioral effects. Some of those can include the following:

- Anxiety and depression: Chronic stress is strongly linked to the development of anxiety and depression. Many studies over the years have been done that show this connection. A more recent article in *Harvard Health Publishing* describes how researchers have gained insight into the long-term effects chronic stress has on our psychological and physical health. Their research "suggests that chronic stress contributes to high blood pressure, promotes the formation of artery-clogging deposits, and causes brain changes that may contribute to anxiety, depression, and addiction."[2] Additionally, preliminary research indicated that chronic stress may contribute to obesity, both directly by causing people to eat more and indirectly due to decreased sleep and exercise.[3]

- Cognitive impairment: Prolonged stress can impair cognitive functions such as memory and concentration, which can include our brain's ability to complete tasks, both simple and complex. According to a 2009 study, stress hormones like cortisol can damage brain structures involved in learning and memory, like the hippocampus.[4]

- Cardiovascular disease: The continuous activation of the stress response can lead to increased heart rate and blood pressure, contributing to cardiovascular disease. One particular updated and highly cited study outlines how stress pathways can lead to atherosclerosis and other cardiovascular conditions.[5]

- Immune system suppression: Studies have shown that chronic and prolonged stress suppresses the immune system and affects its functions, making the body more susceptible to infections and diseases.[6]

- Sleep disturbances: The overproduction of stress hormones can lead to difficulties in sleeping, further exacerbating stress. The American Psychological Association provides many resources and research findings linking stress to sleep problems.
- Substance abuse: Individuals under constant stress may turn to alcohol, drugs, or unhealthy eating habits as coping mechanisms, leading to substance abuse issues. One particular 2008 study out of the New York Academy of Sciences reviewed how stress increases the risk of addiction through its impact on the brain's reward system.[7]

During all these beatings over the years, since my brother and I were the youngest of the brood, we would hide in one of the bedrooms, sitting shivering on the lower bunk bed. We were usually too afraid to even cry, but I could always feel my brother physically shivering next to me. Most of the time, we didn't see the beatings, but we could clearly hear the shouting and screaming, including my older siblings begging and crying for my father to stop the beatings. My mother was no doormat; she often tried hard to fight back, but she was smaller, and my father was extra strong, especially when he was in that rage-filled state of mind. For years, I felt shame and guilt for not helping or at least attempting to stop the beatings like my sisters. In one incident, my father went after my mom with a samurai sword he had hanging in our living room. My sister rushed in and twisted my father's fingers as hard as she could until he dropped the sword and left the room, ending the beating. One rare triumph for my sister!

As my older sisters got married and moved out of the house, my father's rules relaxed, and his physical abuse of my mom became less frequent. Then he was diagnosed with cancer. I would have thought if anything could stop him, it would be cancer. I was wrong. Even when he was in the hospital, he tried to get out of his hospital bed to hit my mom because of something she said. Everyone's excuse was that he was on morphine and so was "not himself." I guess he was not himself for the past fifty years of their marriage! He was not on morphine then!

I hate my father.

Beneath the heavy cloak of hatred for my father, a deeper question lingered, whispering through the anger: how has this traumatic childhood experience shaped who I have become? With these words, I stood on the precipice of an uncharted journey, ready to explore the origins of my being beyond the shadows cast by my father's actions.

CHAPTER 5

Who Am I?

GROWING UP IN SINGAPORE, one of my sisters and I were often seen as different from our other siblings, primarily due to our darker complexions. In a society where beauty standards were heavily influenced by fair skin, we found ourselves labeled as the "ugly" ones within our family. This label was a reflection of the broader cultural preference for lighter skin, a preference that unfortunately led to unfair judgments and categorizations.

To compound matters, I had a personal struggle with excessive sweating, a not uncommon reaction to Singapore's sweltering climate. This natural bodily response, however, became a source of teasing within my family, earning me the nickname "stinky." The combined tags of "ugly" and "stinky" weighed heavily on me, deepening my introverted nature, and severely impacting my self-esteem. As a result, family gatherings became a source of anxiety for me. I would try to blend into the background, hoping to escape any negative attention or comments. This partly helped shape my childhood and adolescence, instilling in me a heightened self-consciousness and a lingering sense of inadequacy. However, these nicknames were not meant to harm but were part of my family's unique, albeit sometimes misguided, way of expressing affection. It was a jesting manner that, while painful at times, was not rooted in malice. I dealt with this by retreating inward and preferring to spend time reading and daydreaming of what life would be like if I lived in the stories I read.

Every year, during school holidays (similar to summer break in the US), one of my sisters and I were sent to spend a couple of weeks with our aunt (our father's sister). Since my sister was my aunt's goddaughter, my mother made sure she had new clothes and shoes to wear during our stays. Our aunt was a schoolteacher and lived on her own. However, she would take us across the street to her best friend's home, and we would spend our entire day there. They often had other friends over to play mahjong, gossip, and eat.

Mahjong is a traditional Chinese tile-based game that has gained widespread popularity in various cultures around the world. The aim of the game is to build a winning hand consisting of a certain number of sets (like the gin rummy card game). Mahjong combines elements of skill, strategy, calculation, and a degree of luck. The game has numerous regional variations, including different scoring rules, tiles, and even play styles. Some of the most popular versions include Chinese mahjong, Japanese riichi mahjong, and American mahjong, each with its own set of rules and styles of play.

When my parents were going through a particularly hard time financially, my father sent my mom to borrow money from my aunt to tide them over for a short period of time. During this time, my mom would bring monthly cash repayments to my aunt. Some months, she would have to apologize that they couldn't make the full regular payment, or sometimes any payment at all. For this reason, my aunt felt she had license to treat my mom however she liked. She also knew my mom didn't have the support of my father. Whenever my aunt came to visit, she would often find fault with something about my mom, be it her cooking, housekeeping, or even the way she dressed—any reason to get on her stream of cursing before she ended her visit. The cursing was especially bad on those occasions when my mom had to apologize for delayed or reduced monthly repayments of the loan.

I didn't like my aunt and dreaded going to her place every year. My aunt's friends would engage my sister in conversation and often compliment her on how pretty she was. As for me, I was known as "the other one." Another innocent remark from one of these friends stayed with me all these years: "I can't believe these two came from the same set of parents!" The only person who paid me any kind attention was my aunt's best friend. She always made sure she spent time with me and that I had enough to eat and drink during mealtimes. I am grateful for her kindness toward me.

My self-image of ugliness was further confirmed in my teenage years. During PE at school, we were asked to walk around the perimeter of the school to warm up before calisthenics in the gym. The PE teacher and one of her favorite students walked together at the back of the class to make sure everyone completed the walk. They were having a good laugh, and when I tuned in on their conversation, I realized they were making fun of the size of my butt! Now I knew I was not just ugly in the face, but my butt was too big as well! I couldn't wait for the walk to be over, and that night, I cried myself to sleep.

Growing up under such scrutiny took a toll on my self-worth. I found it challenging to believe in myself, and my confidence remained elusive. I internalized these hurtful labels, and they became a part of my identity, affecting my interactions with others and my perception of my own self-worth. I unconsciously carried this with me all the way into my adulthood.

The experiences of being labeled as ugly, stinky, and having a big butt during my formative years left lasting scars. But they taught me the importance of empathy and understanding, because appearances and personal hygiene are often beyond an individual's control, especially as a child. They also underscore the need for a supportive environment where children can thrive and build their self-esteem based on their unique qualities and inner worth, rather than superficial judgments. Unfortunately, it took me way too long to overcome this. As mentioned previously, that's one of the reasons why I decided to write this book—to help readers understand that the opinions of others do not define their truth or worth. It was a challenging journey to unlearn these harmful perceptions and rebuild my self-image. Through sharing my story, I hope to inspire others to find the strength to rise above negative labels and embrace their true selves, fostering a world where we judge less and love more.

We as adults need to be sensitive to what we say and do, especially when we are around children. They are always listening and watching. Taking practical steps to address issues related to labeling and self-esteem can make a positive impact on the lives of children and individuals affected by such challenges.

My ways of helping in this are through volunteering at my church and teaching elementary to middle school-age kids in Sunday school. In more recent years, I've also led women's Bible study groups and book clubs at work. In these forums, I have the opportunity to do the following to help promote healthy self-images:

- Be intentional about talking openly about positive body image and share stories of individuals who have overcome body image struggles to inspire and empower both children and adults.
- Teach children about different cultures, ethnicities, and beauty standards to foster acceptance and appreciation of diversity.
- Address bullying and destructive teasing.
- Praise and recognize children for their achievements, talents, and efforts to boost their self-esteem and self-worth instead of focusing on their looks.
- Emphasize that everyone is unique and should embrace their own identity.

Embracing the lessons and strategies shared through my volunteering experiences, you too have the power to make a significant impact. By reading this book, you're equipping yourself with insights and practical guidance that can be applied within your own communities—be it through volunteering, leading discussion groups, or simply engaging in conversations with those around you. Remember, your efforts in fostering a nurturing and inclusive community can ripple outward, touching lives and empowering individuals to embrace their true selves with confidence and pride. Moreover, take this journey beyond the pages. Engage in workshops, online forums, or social media platforms where discussions about self-image and diversity are taking place. Your active participation and the sharing of your own experiences can inspire others to reflect on their perspectives and can foster a more inclusive and empathetic community. By doing so, you are not just following my guidance, you are paving new paths toward acceptance and understanding, one conversation at a time.

What was Life Like Outside the Beatings and Terror?

Growing up, I did have a life outside of the beatings and terror. Looking back, I would say we had two kinds of fun—the one that was organized by my father and the one we had when he was not home. The organized events were few and far between because we simply could not afford to do many of them. Since these outings were rare, we were always excited to be able to go out. Prior to taking us to any movies, my father would take my mom and his mistress to preview a movie to make sure it was appropriate for us. Once a movie was vetted, he would purchase seven tickets for us to go on another day. On the day of the movie, my mom would drive and drop us off at the theater entrance. My oldest sister was given cash to purchase each of us an ice cream cone before we took our seats inside. If someone were to be watching these seven kids politely and quietly sitting in a row, eating their ice cream cones, and waiting for the movie to start, they would think, "How disciplined!" They would have never guessed that we were trained to believe that if we misbehaved, our father would somehow find out.

After the advertisements and trailers would end and the actual movie started, my oldest sister would whisper to the sibling next to her, "Show starting," and this sibling would whisper to the next with those same words, this cadence repeating till it got to the last sibling in the row. I guess she was concerned that some of us were too young to know and may be confused, thinking the previews were part of the movie. I thought it was a cute gesture!

The amusement park was a scary experience for me. My father took us all to one, and the bright and flashing lights, the crowd, and the noise of screaming kids scared me. Screaming to me means someone is afraid, not excited or thrilled! I remember two things about this event, the rest I've blocked out. I was being put on one of the scary-looking wooden horses in the merry-go-round, and I clung on with closed eyes, so afraid that I might slip off. Then, the long silent walk in the dark back to the car for the ride home.

One year, my father arranged for a boat to take us out to sea to look back and watch fireworks on the island. That was an amazing experience. I enjoyed that show, and whenever I watch fireworks, I am always reminded of that night with all of us sitting silently on the boat, rocking gently with the waves, and hearing the loud booming in the distance before each fantastic colorful firework burst into the sky. I love fireworks!

Now what I really enjoyed were the times when my father was not at home. On those days, we didn't have to set the table or even sit there to have our meals. My mom would allow us to try using our hands to eat, just like we'd seen our Malay, Indian, and Peranakan Chinese friends do. She would cook foods that were not considered "proper" for the dinner table, more street food than restaurant-quality. A good example is when she would scald fresh cockles with boiling water, and we would use our hands to pull apart the shells to get to the flesh, dip them in chili sauce, and eat them straight out of the pot! Barbaric, but we loved it! We were allowed to talk with our mouths full, laugh out loud, and tease each other. She even made doing chores fun. During these times, I was totally relaxed, free, and happy!

My father, in his desire to protect us (especially his daughters), created a world where I grew up carefully shielded from the harsh realities of life. In my cocoon of innocence, I was blissfully ignorant of the existence of malevolent individuals who could look you in the eye and deceive you with their lies. I was so sheltered that I didn't even grasp the concept of sex until I reached the age of eighteen. It was during a biology class on the human reproductive system that I mustered the courage to ask a friend next to me, "If the sperm is in the man, and the egg is in the woman, how did the sperm get into the egg?" My innocent inquiry became the subject of ridicule, and I bore the weight of teasing the rest of the school year. My classmates made fun of me, but they never gave me the answer. So, the answer eluded me until that momentous day at eighteen when I finally learned the intricate details of the act, marking the beginning of my journey into a world I had never known before.

CHAPTER 6

I Married My Father!

ALTHOUGH MY FATHER WAS doing better financially when I graduated from high school, he still could not afford to send all his children away to college. The standards for the National University of Singapore were very high, and only the cream of the crop was admitted. Those who did not qualify or have the money would send their kids overseas (usually to the US, Canada, or the UK) for their college education. My father encouraged me to apply to a school in Canada because one of his colleagues was Canadian and had highly recommended a great school there. I meticulously completed the application, wrote and submitted the required essay, and waited impatiently for their response. A couple of months later, to my utter delight, I received their acceptance letter.

The last piece of information they needed was a bank statement. After asking my mom to remind my father several times that I needed this and not getting any responses back, I knew deep down that I wasn't going. I guess my father wanted to give me hope, thinking I would not be accepted anyway. I was a mediocre student at best, and he must have been surprised when I was accepted. Frankly, so was I because, at that time, my self-esteem was so low that I considered myself not just ugly but stupid as well. This incident, a hope so cruelly dashed, was a wound that took a long time to heal. Dashed hope is something I would not wish upon anyone. I clung to that acceptance letter for years, a bitter reminder of what could have been.

Outwardly, resilient as ever, I did what I do best—brushed it aside, put on a happy face, and went out into the workforce. Without a college degree, I started out at the bottom of the ladder in a clerical position. Although a few of my sisters and I were working, we still stayed with our parents. It was expected that we not leave the "nest" until the day we got married—a common practice among a lot of Asian families back in those days.

Since my father couldn't afford to send me away to college, at age eighteen, I found my first job at an Anglo-Dutch company in downtown Singapore. The corporate world, so new and baffling, was also exhilarating. Despite my sheltered upbringing, I found excitement in this unfamiliar territory. My mom still packed my lunch, dropped me off in the morning, and picked me up at the end of each workday. My naivete in this new environment must have been glaringly apparent to my more seasoned colleagues. Thankfully, the executive assistant to the managing director, affectionately known to all as "Mama-san," saw something in me. She took me under her wing, guiding me through the corporate labyrinth. She warned me about the workplace dynamics, especially the unreliability of "what the guys say," and protected me from those she thought might cause me harm. She was the first of many angels in my life.

One day, a salesman visited our office, pitching a course alongside an enticing offer of three free books. Having an insatiable thirst for learning (as I still do to this day), I was attracted by the offer of not just this course but also the three free books that came with it. Oh, how I love free stuff! I promptly signed up and wrote him a check. When Mama-san found out, she went straight to the managing director, Mr. Thomas. He called me into his office to explain that I had been taken in by this salesman, who was essentially just selling the books and not the course, and the "course" that I thought I was purchasing was not worth the money I had paid. He then called this salesman into his office to have a conversation. When the salesman left, Mr. Thomas handed me my check back. I was utterly embarrassed that I could not see through this. It was a hard lesson, teaching me the importance of skepticism and discernment in a world where not everyone's intentions are honest.

Not long after I started working at this Anglo-Dutch firm, a new employee caught everyone's attention. He was tall and handsome, and he carried himself with a charm and charisma that seemed to light up the room. Like many of my female colleagues, I found myself drawn to his magnetic personality. His attention toward me came as a surprise, sparking a whirlwind of emotions. I was smitten, struck hard by Cupid's arrow, and before I knew it, I had fallen head over heels in love with him.

Eager to share this budding romance, I invited him home to meet my parents. My mom was instantly charmed by his charisma and warmth. She saw him as a wonderful match for me and didn't hesitate to express her approval. My father, however, was more discerning. After their meeting, he quietly expressed his reservations to my mom, suggesting that the man might not be "intellectually compatible" with me. His words were a subtle hint of concern, masked in a diplomatic choice of words. He knew instinctively that if he were to outright object, his objections would push me further into the relationship.

Meanwhile, friends at work, including the ever-watchful Mama-san, offered their own warnings. They labeled him a "player," a term I wasn't aware of at that time. But even as I learned what that term implied, my infatuation blinded me to the potential truth behind their cautionary words. I held on to the belief that our love would transform him—that once we were together, he would change for the better, for us. Reflecting on the moment my mom first witnessed my father's violent nature, as he fatally swung a cat by its tail, it dawned on me how love's enchantment and our refusal to see the unpleasant truths can blind us to the true essence of someone's character. I was not totally innocent, and I was warned, but I refused to see it!

Today, I am more cautious and more mindful when cultivating relationships in order to avoid being blinded by love or the unwillingness to see the true nature of someone's character. Here are ten tips that can help guide you:

- Trust your intuition: Pay attention to your gut feelings about a person. If something feels off, don't ignore it. Your intuition is a powerful tool in recognizing warning signs.
- Observe actions, not just words: Actions speak louder than words. Watch how people treat others, especially in situations where they don't stand to gain anything. This can reveal more about a person's character than promises, declarations of love, or loyalty.
- Take time: Don't rush into deep emotional commitments without truly knowing the person. Time reveals

a person's character, especially how they handle stress, disagreements, and adversity.

- Seek honest feedback: Sometimes we're too close to a situation to see it clearly. Trusted friends and family can offer perspectives about your relationship that you might not have considered. Back when I met my ex-husband, I was naive and did not heed the feedback from well-meaning friends. Please keep my hard lesson in mind and don't let that happen to you.

- Educate yourself on red flags: Learn about the red flags of abusive or manipulative behavior. Knowledge of these can help you identify and address concerns early on.

- Maintain independence: Keep your hobbies, friendships, and interests. A healthy relationship should complement your life, not consume it. Independence in a relationship helps you keep a clear perspective.

- Practice self-reflection: Regularly reflect on how you feel about the relationship. Do you feel respected, valued, and heard? Are your needs being met? Self-reflection helps in understanding your feelings and deciding if the relationship is truly beneficial for you.

- Set boundaries: Know your limits and make them clear. Setting healthy boundaries is crucial in any relationship and is a sign of mutual respect and understanding.

- Communication: Cultivate an environment where open and honest communication is encouraged. Being able to discuss concerns, feelings, and needs openly can prevent misunderstandings and build trust.

- Professional guidance: If you're unsure about your feelings or how to interpret someone's behavior, consider seeking advice from a relationship counselor or therapist.

By being mindful of these aspects, you can protect yourself from getting too involved too quickly with someone who may not be showing their true colors and ensure that your relationships are healthy and respectful.

The Fog Clears, Revealing Harsh Truths

Reality soon unfolded in a way that starkly contradicted my fantasies. The relationship, far from being the fairytale I had envisioned, became a lesson in love, trust, and the harsh truths of human nature. My naive belief that love could change a person's fundamental traits was put to the test. Oh boy, was I wrong. I now know a leopard can not change its spots.

Before I knew it, I found myself in the clutches of an abusive marriage—a twisted reality where I believed that the physical torment I endured was just a normal facet of married life. This belief, of course, was based on my only reference point at that time, which was my parents' marriage. The thought of sharing my agony with my family didn't even cross my mind, as the darkness within our home seemed somehow routine. At that time, the narrative I had in my head to make myself feel better was that at least my husband did not beat me as badly as my father beat my mom. I had blindly tied the knot with a man who friends had warned me was a womanizer, but my desperate longing to escape the violent confines of my upbringing led me to ignore their well-intentioned caution. A case of out of the frying pan, into the fire!

I was married but felt utterly alone. I had been entrusted with the upbringing of our daughter and son while their father remained conspicuously absent, never around to provide the support and care we deserved. I was too busy balancing my work life and being there for the children to notice or think much about their father never being there on Saturdays, claiming he had to work all day. The kids and I would usually spend the day enjoying our time with my sisters and the kids' cousins, either at each other's homes or at the swimming club.

An additional challenge I had was our daughter's severe asthma. She was a preemie and born prone to severe asthma attacks. Before the age of three, she was in and out of the hospital many times, adding a layer of despair to my already overwhelming existence. I remember one Lunar New Year's Eve when she had an asthma attack, and assuming her doctor would be celebrating the holiday dinner, I waited to call him. The other fear in my mind was that because it was an auspicious occasion, it would be seen as "bad luck" to talk about taking her to the hospital since my father was highly superstitious and the attack happened right after dinner while we were still at his house. When I could not wait any longer, I took our daughter to the ER, hoping the attending doctor would be able to help her. She was having such a hard time breathing that her fingernails were starting to turn blue due to lack of oxygen. It turned out that her left lung had collapsed, and they had to insert a tube to reinflate it. I got a talking-to from her pediatrician, who said that since she was his worst patient, no matter what time of night or day, I was to call him immediately if something happened. I am so blessed to have had a doctor who really cared about my daughter's welfare.

When she had her more minor attacks, I would sit on the couch in the living room and have her sleep upright on my chest so she could breathe and sleep through the night. These were the nights when I would know exactly what time in the wee hours of the morning their father came home. He always had an excuse, and I think my naive self wanted to believe them, so I did.

One Saturday morning, I sat up in bed and heard my husband in the shower getting ready to go to the office. I heard a still, small voice say, "Something is wrong with your marriage." I was shocked, and I looked around at the empty bedroom. To this day, I do not understand all my actions that followed after hearing this, but I do remember them as clearly as if it was yesterday. It was as if I was on autopilot, guided somehow. On reflection, years later, I believed it was God who had guided me that day. I stood up and got dressed. When my husband came out of the bathroom, he was shocked to see me all dressed up. I told him I needed a ride downtown because my mom needed me to go do something for her. He quietly got dressed and told me I should wait for our daughter to wake up so I could take her with me and that he could meet us for lunch later that day. I bravely said, "No."

He got really angry then, gave me a hard slap, and accused me of being "difficult" when he was trying to do something nice. Somehow, I felt strong and resolved to go downtown. I didn't know why, and I didn't back off either. Like I said, I was on autopilot. At that time, we had a full-time maid who lived with us, so I didn't have a problem leaving and heading downtown. Having a full-time, live-in maid in Singapore was relatively inexpensive. We imported these workers (domestic help, construction and factory workers, etc.) from countries like the Philippines, China, and India. These foreign workers were hired through specialized agencies, and we put up a bond as insurance that they would not break the law.

He drove like the devil, dropped me off at my office (since all the shops downtown were still closed), and sped off. I found out later that his Saturday routine was to pick up his mistress, have breakfast with her, go to the office to work for a couple of hours, and then spend the rest of the day with her. I had unknowingly disrupted his routine rendezvous.

I was still on autopilot. I went up to my office and called one of my sisters to tell her about the voice I heard and my husband's odd behavior that morning. The insidious truth finally emerged when she told me that she believed he was having an ongoing affair. That explained his behavior that day, and it was as if a veil was lifted from my eyes. I suddenly realized that he wasn't around much, and all those late nights and full workdays on Saturdays were clear signs I felt so stupid to not have seen.

I agonized over what to do. As you know, I am a Christian, and as such, I was advised I must try to preserve the marriage because divorce was not "a good Christian thing to do." However, in the back of my mind, I told myself that, unlike my mother, who had no choice, I did have a choice, and I was not going to share my husband with anyone! That is the stubborn streak in me that would serve me well later in this journey. I saw how living in a fractured marriage environment destroyed me as a child, and I was not about to do the same to my own children. So, to compromise, I agreed to at least give him a chance to repent and make this right.

Later that week, I confronted him about his ongoing affair. He said it was nothing serious, and he promised to end the illicit relationship immediately, setting the stage for the worst three months of my life. I told him if he was serious about reconciling and working together to improve our relationship going forward, then I was game, on the condition that if I were to find out the affair was still ongoing, or if there were any other affairs in the future, it would be the end of our marriage. He agreed. I am so glad I laid down those ground rules. I watched in agony as he continued his affair, leaving the house for supposed evening jogs at 5 p.m. only to return at 3 a.m.—his alibi a cruel joke. I thought to myself, *He must think I am stupid!* I realized he would never willingly admit the affair was still ongoing unless I caught him with the woman.

After three months of agony, I was ready for this to be over. While I waited for an opportunity to confirm my suspicions, I started looking into how I could keep the children, should I find myself going down the divorce track. I was told by an attorney friend at that time that when a parent can show evidence that the spouse committed adultery, the court will automatically award full custody of any children to the noncheating parent. I was happy to hear that there was a way to make sure I got full custody of the children; that was my priority.

I hired a private investigator. I figured that whatever evidence he gathered, I could still choose whether or not to use it later. Better to have a choice than none at all—that was important to me. It didn't take long before this investigator sent me his report on all the evidence he had collected. I wasn't surprised at what I saw in the report because I knew in my heart the affair was ongoing, and the report just confirmed it for me. The private investigator told me his services included his appearance in court to testify on my behalf. The ball was now in my court to take this further or drop it.

A few weeks later, my opportunity came one day when my husband told me he was going fishing with our brother-in-law that evening. Other than the open seas, there are many commercial fishing areas inland where Singaporeans go to fish. These commercial "ponds" are stocked with fish, making them more attractive to customers. I called my sister and asked if she could be on the lookout when my husband picked up my brother-in-law to see if the girlfriend was in the car. When my husband saw my sister waiting outside with her husband, he swerved his car and turned on the high beams to blind her so she would not be able to see inside the car. However, when he swerved, my sister, for a brief moment, did see a woman in the car. Once I confirmed she would be there, I knew this was my one opportunity to catch him with her and end this pain.

The only other person who had been fishing at these commercial ponds with my husband was my brother. I called him to ask if he knew which of these they were most likely to be at. Since he had no idea what was going on, I explained the situation to him.

I could not take any more of the excuses or the pain. My brother picked me up, and we went to a couple of these places before we saw my husband's car parked at one of them. Except for some lanterns used by the fishermen around the pond, the place was pitch black. Then we saw them, and they saw us. I was curious to know what the woman looked like, so I tried to walk up to her to have a better look. My husband thought I was going to do something to her and put out his hand to stop me in my tracks. Once he did that, my brother jumped into action to protect me. I quickly told them that I was not there to fight; my purpose was to let my husband know I was aware the affair was still going on and that he knew what that meant. With that, my brother and I turned around and left and he drove me home.

When I got home, I packed my husband's things into two suitcases and left them just inside the front door. I stayed up all night reflecting on my life. Till then, I had lived a life of naivety, and that night I grew up. I knew I had two children who depended on me, and it was up to me to do the very best I could to give them a good life. The next morning, I left the house early and went to work. My maid told me my husband had come home midmorning, saw the suitcases, picked them up, turned around, and left. I came home from work that day and felt a sense of relief. It was as if a great weight had been lifted off my chest and I could breathe again. I was heartbroken, but I no longer had to listen to all the excuses and lies or deal with the often alternating feelings of anxiousness, anger, and sadness while waiting for him to come home. For him, he was now free to have as many girlfriends and go on as many "evening jogs" as his heart desired.

In the meantime, I filed for divorce and waited for a court date.

Keeping Secrets is a Big Killer

Keeping painful secrets locked away, whether they be from growing up in a violent household or enduring an abusive and unfaithful husband in adulthood as I have, is not healthy and can have serious consequences, both emotionally and physically. It's crucial to recognize the impact of silence and take steps to break free from the cycle of abuse.

Here are some of the consequences I suffered from keeping my secrets locked in for so many years:

- Emotional turmoil: Holding onto these painful secrets led me to a constant state of emotional turmoil. Staying silent is a heavy burden, resulting in anxiety, depression, and low self-esteem. The longer these secrets remain hidden, the more damaging the emotional toll becomes.

- Isolation: The shame and fear associated with these experiences often kept me in isolation. I withdrew from friends, believing that if they found out who I really was, they would steer clear of me. I felt very alone in my suffering.
- Physical health issues: The stress of keeping these secrets can take a toll on physical health, leading to various health problems. I suffered from insomnia, high blood pressure, chronic headaches, and other aches and pains.
- Lack of self-worth: I didn't think much of myself and had lost what little sense of self-worth I may have had, believing there was something wrong with me because I seemed to attract bullies. I must not be able to see it, but others could see it in me.

Recognizing the signs of abuse and its impact is a pivotal first step toward liberation. If you're reading this and see echoes of your own experiences in my story, know that acknowledgment is the gateway to breaking the cycle. You've already begun the journey by understanding that silence only perpetuates the cycle of abuse. Later in the book, I will share some action steps you can take to break free and start healing. The journey is undoubtedly challenging, but it is also filled with hope. Each step you take toward healing is a testament to your strength and resilience. Remember, moving out of the shadow of abuse and into the light of recovery begins with a single brave step. You have the power and the will to forge a new path, one where your voice is heard and your life is your own.

CHAPTER 7

Alone but Free

MY NOW EX-FATHER-IN-LAW, A fellow worker bee of bustling downtown Singapore, and I shared a bond forged by heartache. Our paths would serendipitously cross during lunch breaks, but the encounters were far from ordinary. His eyes would betray the turmoil within as he inquired about the children and me, his voice quivering with the weight of unshed tears. Witnessing his profound sadness cut me deeply and was a stark reminder of the collateral damage inflicted by the separation. His love for me and his grandchildren was palpable, as he continuously offered heartfelt apologies for what his son had done. Seeing him in such a state hurt because I loved him very much.

In his earnest attempt to mend what was broken, he would offer well-intentioned advice. He encouraged me to be more demonstrative in my affection toward my now ex-husband, citing a grievance that had been aired. Apparently, my ex-husband had complained about the absence of those little gestures of love—like holding hands when exiting the car—that his girlfriend so readily bestowed upon him. I couldn't help but retort with a touch of sarcasm, suggesting that I'd have my three-year-old daughter tend to her one-year-old brother whenever we got out of the car. This, I jestingly argued, would free me up to lovingly clasp my ex-husband's hand.

After all, wasn't this the reason he sought the companionship of a girlfriend?

But amid the well-intentioned advice and humorous comebacks, there lingered a wound that cut deeper for me than any words ever could. The most piercing blow was my ex-husband's declaration that he had "never loved me." I found myself bewildered by the paradox of a marriage devoid of love. It begged the question—why would he marry someone he claimed never to have loved? There was no impending financial gain, no shotgun wedding forced by an unexpected pregnancy. It was an enigma I couldn't unravel. My ex-father-in-law tried to comfort me by saying that his son had to find an excuse for his bad behavior in order to assuage his own guilt. This made me think that my father married my mother because of a bet with his friends, and he clearly did not love her. No one can beat a woman for over fifty years and love her at the same time! What was my ex-husband's story that made him marry me when he had "never loved me?" Did he also have a bet with his friends that he would get "the good girl?"

Regrettably, the separation did not also end the harassment that my ex-husband decided to inflict upon me. It became persistent, growing more vicious with time. These encounters often took place in the late hours of the night, with him inebriated and full of rage. He would pound on my apartment door, his curses echoing through the night, waking our children up in terror. There was no way I would allow this to continue, and I knew I had to do something to stop it. I had experienced firsthand the fear of being abruptly awakened from a peaceful slumber by the sounds of violence, and I would not subject my children to any of it.

The following day, after another of these incidents, I called him and arranged to meet him after work. As we sat down and began to talk, the truth unfolded. He had lost his job, he said, pointing an accusatory finger at me. He held me responsible for his failed job interviews, where people who knew us and were aware of our separation had inquired about my well-being. To his dismay, these interviews never culminated in job offers, leaving him bitter and convinced that I had been painting him in a negative light, poisoning our mutual acquaintances' perception of him. In reality, I had not mentioned what had happened to anyone who asked because I believed he was doing a great job of showing what kind of a man he was all by himself, exhibiting unfaithful behaviors out in public. In contrast, I was known as the "good girl" in the industry. My prayer throughout this ordeal was to leave God to deal with my ex-husband as He saw fit. All I asked was that God protect me and my children, and He has!

I also learned that his girlfriend had left him. This did not come as a surprise to me since many affairs thrive on secrecy and the excitement of forbidden romance. When the affair is exposed, the secrecy disappears, and with it, the thrill that often fuels such relationships. Some individuals engage in affairs for excitement and novelty, and once that's gone, they quickly lose interest.

During this difficult conversation, I offered him a piece of advice that would eventually lead to a turning point. I suggested he approach a dear friend who managed a car dealership to explore the possibility of a sales position. Although he had no experience in sales, I believed his natural charisma and charm could make him an exceptional salesman. To my surprise, he heeded my advice and secured a job at the dealership. As a result, the midnight harassment ceased, providing much-needed relief for me and the children.

My dear readers, I told you I grew up the night I packed my ex-husband's bags, and you can see here that I did. When our backs are pushed against the wall and our circumstances seem dire, that is the time we need to evoke our iron will within, be creative, and think of ways we can work around the situation. Putting our heads down and shrinking into ourselves, thinking there is nothing we can do, is self-defeating. For me, I took a bold step and engaged my ex-husband in a civil, mature conversation, giving me an opportunity to find out more about what was happening. I saw an opening to help him with a suggestion on his job hunt during this conversation. Necessity is the mother of invention.

However, amid the turmoil of unemployment, a shocking act further tested the bounds of reason and decency. On one fateful afternoon while I was at work, he surreptitiously threatened my maid into allowing him to enter my apartment and ransack it, pilfering everything of value. My cherished jewelry and an ornate Venetian vase were among the casualties of his avarice. He probably wanted my jewelry, so he had something valuable to give to his girlfriend in his efforts to keep the relationship alive.

Overwhelmed by anger and betrayal, I made the difficult decision to call my ex-father-in-law, bearing the heavy burden of delivering the news of his son's actions. I couldn't help but highlight the depths of his son's callousness, sarcastically telling him that the only thing he had forgotten to take during his plunder was his children's food from the pantry. Surely he could have sold it so as to continue affording his girlfriend.

The theft was an infuriating betrayal, but it also served as a confirmation for me that I had made the right decision to sever ties with such a man. He not only failed to provide any financial support for his children but had the audacity to also steal from their mother—the very person working tirelessly to provide for them. It was a painful lesson that reinforced the importance of protecting oneself and one's loved ones, especially in the face of betrayal and adversity.

The way I got past this was by reminding myself of a vital truth—material possessions can be replaced. What truly mattered, above all else, was the safety and well-being of my children. No matter what harm my ex-husband chose to inflict on me in the present and in the future, one thing remained unassailable—my children were securely with me. This unwavering certainty became my North Star, guiding me through the darkest of times.

In the initial months following the separation, a painful routine emerged. The children would spend either Saturday or Sunday with their father each week, and it was a heart-wrenching sight to witness. My son, grappling with his inner turmoil, would cry and plead to not go with him every single time. My daughter, on the other hand, divulged a disturbing truth—her father would discipline her brother by striking him with a rolled-up newspaper or magazine whenever he cried during their time together. She didn't want to be beaten, so, she told me, she was brave and didn't cry. When my son was a baby, and while waiting for me to warm up his milk, his father would go to the crib and smack him a few times in an attempt to stop him from crying. I believe having to manage living a double life at that time would have been frustrating and stressful, but though that was the state of mind he was in, it does not excuse his abusive behavior. He was taking his frustrations out on his baby son, and his son feared him.

Then one day, an epiphany struck me like a bolt of lightning. I told my ex-husband that until he could help me support the kids financially, he should not be granted the privilege of spending time with them. Remarkably, he readily agreed to this arrangement, allowing me to regain a modicum of control over our lives. It was a crucial step forward, one that relieved our family of the weekly struggle and spared my children from the anguish of being torn away from their mother to spend time with a man they hardly knew but feared.

It was quite bewildering. I could understand a man not wanting to have anything to do with his ex-wife but couldn't fathom a father who would willingly distance himself from his own children. It was a powerful testament to my ex-husband's self-centered nature—an individual perpetually driven by his own desires.

This experience showed me a valuable lesson. As I mentioned earlier, we should never shy away from taking steps to alleviate pain, stress, frustrations, or even fear, both for ourselves and our loved ones. In this instance, my ex-husband knew that, based on accepted legal visitation rights, I couldn't prevent him from seeing his children. However, he was happy that I gave him "permission" and a reason not to feel obligated to see his children, relieved of the burden of accommodating them during his outings with his girlfriend. It was a victory for me, sparing my children from the weekly turmoil of spending a day with their father. It also helped me by alleviating my anxieties, as I would wonder all day how they were doing when they were out with their father.

When I discovered that he had encouraged my children

to call his girlfriend "mommy" during one of their outings, I drew a firm line. I reminded him that any woman could claim the title of his wife, but none could ever be the mother to my children. In response, anger flared across his face, and he reached out to grab ahold of me. Instinctively, I fled toward the dining room, urging our maid to pick up my son as I passed. She shielded my son with her own body as my ex-husband stepped on her back to get to me. He grabbed the nearby desk phone (yes, those existed at that time) and smashed it into my head with a loud crack. As blood poured from the gash on my forehead, he took his anger out on me some more. I could smell alcohol on his breath, and I remember thinking, *Why is he drinking at this time of the day?* The smell of alcohol on someone's breath immediately brings back this memory for me.

As the assault raged on, he vented his fury upon me, leaving me battered and bruised. I sat down on the cold marble floor, stunned and bleeding. A deafening silence enveloped the room. Then I heard a chair scraping. I turned to see my four-year-old daughter, displaying a maturity beyond her years, begin picking up the toppled dining room chairs, one by one. The chairs were taller than she was, but she fastidiously went around picking each one up and set it back in place around the table. She then turned her attention to our maid, who sat stunned on the kitchen floor, holding onto my son. My daughter calmly instructed her to "fetch my mommy some bandages, as her head is bleeding." In that moment, I wept. I was ashamed. My four-year-old was forced by these circumstances into the role of an adult, while I, her mother, sat on the floor, numb.

To this day, I remain eternally grateful to our maid, a strong twenty-two-year-old young woman. She had shielded my son from harm with her own body and suffered bruises on her back. I shudder to think of the consequences if she had not intervened. His delicate bones could have been crushed, his fragile lungs punctured if his strong, five-foot-eleven, 140-pound father had stepped on him to get to his mother. The next day, I took immediate action, instructing my lawyer to file a restraining order. Never again would I allow my children to witness such violence.

This experience underscored a vital truth—children absorb and remember everything, even at a tender age. My son's memory of that traumatic incident resurfaced years later, a stark reminder of the lasting impact of our actions and choices. In a candid moment with his cousins, he expressed a sentiment that left everyone at the table in stunned silence. He vowed that when he grew up, he would buy a gun and kill his father. When questioned about his reasons, he simply stated, "Because he hit my mommy on her head with the phone." It was a poignant reminder that children bear the scars of their past, even when they may appear to have moved on.

While my days were dark, and my nights even darker, I dug deep, looking for a way to overpower and rise above this darkness. I knew this to be possible and that no one could do it for me. A flicker of resolve sparked within me—a silent vow that I would find a way out of this. Little did I know this ember of determination would soon ignite a daring journey beyond borders, leading me to a place where I could seek refuge and rebuild my life for my children and myself.

CHAPTER 8

The Escape

DEALING WITH THE PAIN of betrayal was just the beginning. As a single mom, I faced not only emotional turmoil but also the weight of social expectations. Our weekly Sunday gatherings at my parents' house became a vivid reminder of my situation. My father, in an attempt to spare my feelings, would warn my sisters not to sit with their husbands during dinner, making the atmosphere uncomfortably tense. Everyone seemed to tiptoe around me, accentuating my sense of isolation. There was no way I could avoid going to these gatherings, so I gutted it out and left as soon as dinner was over, every single time.

Despite my financial independence, my parents worried incessantly. They would make unannounced visits to stock my pantry, refrigerator, and freezer. While well-intentioned, it often made me feel ashamed that I had put them through the worry and stress. My mom's constant reminders about the need for me to find a companion "for when the kids are grown" only added to the pressure. It also made me wonder whether that was the reason she stayed in an abusive relationship for over fifty years; was it because she did not want to be alone when we were all grown and had left the nest?

This brings up the memory of a conversation some of my siblings and I had with my mom. It is customary for Buddhists to "send" luxury things with their loved ones when they pass away or in remembrance of their passing during the seventh month of the lunar calendar. The way these are sent is by burning things like paper money, beautifully constructed paper houses or cars, and so forth. We were lightheartedly discussing with my mom what she would like us to send with her when she died. She told us we don't have to send her a house because she will be living with my father in his house. It shocked us all that she still wanted to live with a husband who abused her for over fifty years! By then, my father had passed away. This either showed the level and depth of the psychological and emotional impact of the abuse made her feel worthless and incapable of surviving alone or living independently or that she still had feelings of love and attachment toward my father.

Avoiding calls from my ex-father-in-law was another source of stress that had become a habit, especially before public holidays. The thought of facing my ex-husband and subjecting my children to potential discomfort and nervousness was unbearable. This avoidance of both men, however, was a double-edged sword, contributing to more stress.

In retrospect, I realize the importance of setting boundaries with family and even ex-family members. Clear communication about my needs and limits could have alleviated some of the stress and helped me maintain a sense of control over my life.

The emotional toll of betrayal never seemed to wane. In the whirlwind of securing my children's custody and escaping a toxic marriage, I neglected to check in on my emotional well-being. However, in my quiet moments, usually in the dead of night, I found myself, as a Christian, questioning God, asking Him why He was putting me through so much pain. I told God I knew there had to be a purpose. I begged Him to reveal it to me. If there were lessons He wanted me to learn, I wanted to know what they were so I could learn and fix them, thinking that would make the pain go away. I heard nothing—silence. So, as always, I soldiered on while waiting, stuffing all the pain inside, deep inside. Outwardly, I moved on. I'm good at putting up a brave front. And though I knew I couldn't take much more of this pain, I knew I didn't have to think about it and could always figure it out later. It would be more than thirty years before my purpose was revealed to me. More about that later in the book.

Professionally, working for an offshore bank with a head office in Dallas, Texas, presented a unique opportunity. I saw this as a potential solution to get away from all the pressures. After a sleepless night, I went into my boss's office the next morning and asked him if the bank would give me a job in Dallas, were I to move there. Knowing my personal situation, my boss readily said yes and that he would give me a good recommendation. He also cautioned me that there was a high level of interest in relocation opportunities to the head office, especially from the UK office. With the low probability of getting approval, I kept this relocation idea to myself. But despite the slim chances, my application was surprisingly approved very quickly. My visa was approved for work in the Dallas office for three years. My boss gave me a month to move. Oh my God, relocation usually takes at least three to six months, and I had one! I knew I had to let my parents know right away.

My family's reaction to my decision to move was varied and complex. My mother told me that if any of her children could do this, it would be me. My mom's belief in me boosted my confidence. She saw in me what she called "the stubbornness" that she had in handling life situations: never allowing road-blocks to defeat me, and instead, always being able to find a way around them. My father, perhaps misunderstanding my intentions, assured me that they would take care of my children while I was in Dallas for the three years. He seemed to assume that I would leave my children behind, focusing on the opportunity for me as an individual. However, my mother made it clear that the move was an all-or-nothing deal for me. I would never leave my children behind. The move, if it were to happen, would include all three of us as a family unit.

This clarification set the tone for the flurry of preparations that followed. It was a period marked by rapid decisions and actions, a dynamic that, in hindsight, was incredibly ben-eficial. The lack of time to overthink the move shielded me from the paralysis of fear and uncertainty. It pushed me into action, forcing me to focus on the practicalities of relocating and setting up a new life in a new country. I had a home to sell, and what was I going to do with all the furniture and things in it? Just like I was at the start of this journey, after I heard that voice in my head, I was purely operating on autopilot, guided somehow from one step to the next.

In this frantic period, I realized the value of decisiveness and the strength of a mother's commitment to her children. The move was not just a change of location; it was a leap of faith, driven by the desire to provide a better life for my family. It was a testament to the resilience and adaptability required of a single parent, facing not just the challenge of starting anew but also the responsibility of ensuring the well-being of my children in an unfamiliar environment.

I left Singapore on a bright, sunny day with my entire life packed into two suitcases, my seven-year-old daughter and five-year-old son in tow along with my mother, whom my father had asked to accompany us to Dallas until we got settled. It was a long, grueling journey. To get to Dallas, including layovers, took twenty-six hours.

Settling in Plano, a suburb of Dallas, meant a whole new set of routines and challenges. Once the kids got settled in at school and I had arranged day care for them, my mom went home. Juggling work in downtown Dallas with the responsibilities of single parenthood was a new experience for me. The unreliable bus system often made me late for day care pickups. The day care charged a dollar a minute when parents were late in picking up their children, and I was close to the day care kicking us out. In Singapore, I'd had a full-time maid who took care of the children while I was at work. As always, I reminded myself I could figure this out; I learned quickly to adjust my schedule to fit into this new way of life.

Life in Plano as a single mom with two children under the age of seven was a journey filled with challenges, growth, and unexpected humor. One evening, after a dinner party, I found myself hilariously lost due to my notorious lack of sense of direction as a driver. One of the VPs at the bank, knowing I was alone in Dallas with no family, invited me to join him and his family and a few friends for dinner close to downtown Dallas. It was still light when I drove there with the kids, so I made it with no issues. However, when I left, it was dark. And since I was unfamiliar with the road system in addition to having to adapt to driving on the other side of the road (Singapore driver seats are on the right side of the car), I quickly found myself completely lost. I stopped a couple of times at the 7-Eleven to ask for directions. I figured if I could find my way to Highway 75, I would know the way home from there. It seemed like I was driving around in circles for several more hours. The kids were asleep in the backseat, and there I was, nowhere near Highway 75! When I told my colleague about this adventure, I explained that when I got lost in Singapore, I would drive around until I got to a place I was familiar with and proceed to my ultimate destination from there. This colleague cautioned me that this strategy would not work in Dallas. If I were to continue to drive around in Dallas like I did in Singapore, I would end up in Mexico! This incident, while funny, underscored the newness of my surroundings and the need for me to adapt quickly.

The day care my children attended presented its own set of challenges. The workers at the day care were the problem. One of them would call my son "Chink" and another bullied my daughter into handing over her handheld computer game. Navigating these difficult situations taught me the importance of advocating for my children and the value of open communication with care providers. The administrator at the day care dealt with the name-calling situation, but the one who had stolen the computer game quit and never returned to the day care after the theft.

After the bad experiences with the day care center, I approached my neighbor to ask if she would (for a fee) pick up the children from school while she was picking up her own child. She agreed, and both my daughter and son became latchkey kids. I would call in the afternoon to make sure they were home and had locked the door behind them. This went on for a while until they decided to ride their bikes to school instead of having to ride home with the neighbor. Our neighbor was quite irresponsible, so I agreed. She was constantly late in picking up the children. In addition, she would change the place where she would pick them up and expect her daughter to let my son and daughter know. This made for a stressful end to their school day, trying to determine where to go and running around looking for her car. Just like their mom, my children had to grow up and adjust quickly to their new environment. It was not easy for them, even though they spoke and understood English perfectly. I can imagine it being even harder for children from other countries who immigrated to the US having not learned to speak English. I am so proud of my children for their tenacity and grit.

My children faced their struggles in school too. After a few weekends of having to visit the eye clinic to get my daughter's glasses adjusted, she finally confessed that a boy in her class would swipe the glasses off her face every time he walked by her. Ironically, this boy was the school counselor's son. I could have gone to see this school counselor to have her son stop this bullying, but I preferred to teach my daughter to stand up for herself. We worked together on strategies to handle this boy, empowering her to stand up for herself.

My son, when in kindergarten, exhibited behaviors indicative of an abused child, a deeply concerning issue. Teachers observed his fear, especially of adult males. During recess, he would stand apart from other children, though he enjoyed watching them play around. When he would notice a teacher, or any male adult, looking at him, he would turn and shy away. When an adult asked him to stop doing something (it didn't even have to be a harsh reprimand), he would immediately crawl under a table or chair and hide there. When the adult would ask him why he was hiding, he would say because the adult said they didn't love him. I explained to them that his father would hit him when he cried and he had developed a fear of him. Collaborating closely with a school counselor, we supported him through dealing with his traumas, leading to a clean bill of health in second grade. These experiences highlighted the need for patience, understanding, and the willingness to seek professional help when necessary.

Going through these counseling sessions with the school counselor for my son, I learned a valuable lesson from her that you might find useful. Throughout the entire journey—finding out about my ex-husband's affairs, the divorce, the harassment, and the move to Dallas—I had kept up a strong front. I didn't allow anyone to see me sad or crying. I did that in the quiet moments when I was alone, usually deep into the night when the children were asleep. The school counselor advised me to feel free to express my hurt and sadness, even in the presence of my children. She said that my children needed to know that the situation had hurt me deeply and this openness would, in turn, help them be open with me about how they were feeling, not just about their biological father but about everything else that was happening in their lives. That was very good advice!

I am very proud of both my children. From a young age, they were able to stand up for themselves and decide to depend on themselves rather than be subjected to the whims of others.

I sincerely believe that I would not have made it in life without "angels" who appeared or were placed by my higher power at critical moments to offer support and guidance. It started with Mama-san at my first job. Then the late Ron H., who protected me at the office in Singapore when my ex-husband came to threaten and harass me there on numerous occasions. Stan played a crucial role in getting me approved for the relocation and helping to secure my US work visa. Nick's compassion was evident when he agreed to hire me for the position in Dallas, and he also gave me a raise upon learning about my housing struggles, ensuring I could afford our apartment in Plano. Ed offered me the opportunity to head up the sales and operations of their first branch in Dallas, a turning point in my career. Finally, Nick S. entrusted me with my first executive role, heading up a procurement and vendor management organization with a spend budget of $2.2 billion, which catapulted my career forward. These angels were more than just bosses and colleagues; they were pivotal in my journey toward stability and success.

When I first moved to the US with my two children, the initial wave of optimism gradually gave way to doubt and uncertainty. About five months in, I was hauling a load of laundry down the stairs of my second-floor apartment to the common laundry room in my apartment complex. It was very cold that day and I slipped on the ice that had formed on the stairs. I sprained my ankle, and for the first time since my move to the US, tears sprang to my eyes and I questioned my decision to relocate. I'd had a pretty comfortable life in Singapore. I had a good income and a live-in maid to take care of everything from babysitting the children to cooking, cleaning, and even shopping. All I had to do was go to work, come home, and enjoy my time with the children. I'd also had the support of my parents there, locally. Here I was on my own. What was I doing here? I allowed myself to wallow in self-pity for a couple of hours; I then dried my eyes and reminded myself of the pain, the harassment from my ex-husband, and the endless stress back home. It seemed to me that my troubles in the US were nothing compared to that mental torture! It may have been hard to get used to having all the responsibilities on my shoulders, but I knew I would get used to this lifestyle soon enough because I was not afraid of hard work. The children and I were safe and could live without harassment from their father, and that was my primary reason for relocating. I took a deep breath, knowing I had indeed made the right decision. The rest I would be able to figure out.

Adapting to the American way of life came with its unique challenges, like, as I mentioned earlier, learning to drive on the other side of the road. It was a disorienting experience at first, symbolizing the larger adjustment to a new way of life. It wasn't just mastering the traffic rules; it was about navigating a new cultural landscape. I had an International Driving Permit that allowed me to drive temporarily in the US. However, I did have to take and pass the driving test in Dallas to get a license to drive in the US and the state of Texas. Out of the kindness of his heart, the person at the DMV looked at me at the end of the driving test and said, "I know you can drive since you have an International Driving Permit, so I am going to give you a pass because you need it." Thank you! He must have sensed my desperation to get this ticked off my list of things I had to get done.

I didn't have a problem when there were other cars on the road. All I needed to do was follow the flow of the traffic. However, when I was driving the kids to day care, we usually left pretty early so I could make it to work on time, and there were hardly any cars out at that time of the morning. One day, a car came straight at me—I was happily traveling on the wrong side of the road! Needless to say, I quickly corrected, changed lanes, and went on my merry way. The other driver probably thought I was drunk.

Another incident caught me off guard. I was walking toward a mall one evening and had to wait for a truck to pass me before I could head to the front door of the mall. The driver of the truck slowed down, rolled down his window, and shouted, "Go back to your own country!" This man was obviously having a bad day! I was shocked, and I wondered to a colleague the next day how this man knew I was from another country. My colleague laughed and educated me on discrimination in America. This man was harassing me purely because I was not white. Singapore is a multicultural society, with all races and nationalities from all over the world living harmoniously in this melting pot. Sure, there are minor discriminations but not as blatant as what I've witnessed here. Such experiences were jarring, challenging my sense of belonging in this new land.

Being stereotyped is another common experience I've had. One particularly amusing incident happened when I was volunteering at a church library after Sunday morning service. My sister was visiting me from Singapore, and I brought her to church with me. When I introduced her to the librarian, the librarian stood up, bowed, and, at the top of her voice, very slowly said, "W-e-l-c-o-m-e t-o A-m-e-r-i-c-a a-n-d t-o o-u-r l-i-b-r-a-r-y." This pattern of speech continued for the duration of our time there. Afterward, my sister and I had the best laugh. I think the librarian immediately assumed that since my sister is from Singapore, she didn't understand English. The irony of this is that 90 percent of Singaporeans are educated in the Queen's English (we were a British colony), and the official language in Singapore is English. Our high school certification comes directly from England and reads, "The Cambridge School Certificate." My sister worked at the Singapore American School and had interacted and communicated with American administrators, teachers, and students for the past ten years! The best part was that the librarian almost screamed out all her words. So apparently, my sister not only didn't understand English but was also deaf. It had to be one of the funniest things that happened to me in those early days. We know the librarian did this unconsciously, and suspect she was just stereotyping Asians as a whole, but no harm, no foul.

I later watched the original *Rush Hour*, where an LAPD detective played by Chris Tucker works with an inspector from Hong Kong played by Jackie Chan. When Chris Tucker meets Jackie Chan for the first time, he shouts at the top of his voice, "Do you understand the words that are coming out of my mouth?" I laughed hard because it reminded me of this experience with the church librarian and my sister! I know this is as real as it gets. In this movie, Jackie's character could speak English, but Tucker's character automatically assumed he couldn't. Let's all be mindful of what hidden biases and microaggressions may be lurking in our subconscious and not jump to conclusions about any behavior traits of other races.

On a darker note, another incident that was a total surprise to me was when we went to visit a Baptist church in Dallas on a Sunday morning. My children and I walked into the small auditorium and were met with a lot of silent stares. From the time we walked into this church until we left, no one spoke to or even smiled at us. I found this rather odd until I noticed that there was not a single non-white person in the congregation. I got the message that we were not welcome there, so I never returned. It is churches like this one that ruined the reputation for genuine Christians.

I am not naive in this respect. I do recognize there is real racial discrimination here in the US and around the world. Like the belief that people from China brought COVID-19 to the US and, therefore, all Chinese people killed a relative, friend, etc., leading strong, healthy males to beat up old Asian women. Or the idea that my husband cheated on me, so all men are cheaters. I even heard a mother's advice to her daughter that "all men eventually beat their wives." Those who speak with a French or Italian accent are so delightful and charming, but others with an accent cannot speak proper English. When we look for discrimination, we will always find it.

The point is, if we feel the need to punish someone, first make sure they indeed committed the crime we think they did. Did the Chinese bring COVID-19 to the US? Maybe, but did the old Asian woman innocently walking on the sidewalk bring it? Did that man you are about to marry beat his ex-wife? Maybe, so find out before you commit to marrying him. Did the author have an accent? Maybe, but find out if she speaks English before you assume she doesn't. I do have a Singaporean accent, and I do speak English . . . very well in fact.

Stepping into the world of corporate America was another significant pivot. To navigate this new terrain demanded more than just professional acumen; it required an intricate dance of adapting to unspoken norms, deciphering the subtle dynamics of power and politics, and finding my voice amid the cacophony of ambition and competition. This part of my life was not just about career growth but a profound lesson in resilience, grit, and the art of balancing my integrity with the demands of an unfamiliar corporate culture.

Life in Corporate America

Life in corporate America felt like a maze of roadblocks, each one testing my resolve and adaptability. Someone I once worked for and respected told me that facing opposition in the workplace often means you're making an impact. If you are not making an impact in an organization, no one will bother to pay you any attention or give you a hard time. They do it because, for some reason, they see you as a threat. This insight was a revelation, helping me see the challenges not as personal attacks but as indicators of my influence and success.

Yes, bullies are there in the workplace as well. It is especially difficult to deal with them when your boss is the bully. When I worked for one of *Fortune* magazine's "Most Admired Companies," I reported to a bully. He would scream, shout, and threaten his team. He was especially harsh and critical with female team members and colleagues. On one occasion, a trip he had asked me to make was canceled after I had already made travel and hotel arrangements. I could easily cancel the hotel, but airlines will usually give you credit you can use for a future flight instead of refunding the cost. I expensed the airfare that I had already paid out, but he refused to approve the refund. The fifth time I asked him, he told me, "You are on your own on that one;" in other words, I had to pay for it! And I did; I paid the $500! That is how intimidated I was by him. When I casually mentioned it to another manager, she was flabbergasted; she immediately escalated the issue up the chain. I was unaware that my boss was already under investigation because his colleagues had filed a complaint about his tactics. My expense report was approved shortly after.

In another incident, this same boss asked me to print out a copy of a report, which I already had a hard copy of, so promptly handed it to him. He said there was a crease on it and wanted me to print him a fresh copy. I looked, but he had not sent me an electronic copy. I told him I didn't have it. He came literally within an inch of my face, pointed his finger at me, and threatened, "If I find that I had sent you a copy later today . . ." I did not let him finish his threat. I piped up and said, "If you find it, I will buy you lunch." I don't know where I got the courage to spout that out in response, but it did the trick. He backed off, turned, and walked away. I think he was so shocked at my response that he didn't know how to react. I think he expected me to cower and apologize. Instead, I conjured up an unflattering image of myself giving him the finger in my mind that got me laughing. I'm quite sure we've all done something similar at some point in our lives. We have to find the humor in order to keep our sanity!

Seriously though, this was another boost to my confidence and a reminder I quickly logged in my mind that I could handle bullies—another quick win added to my mental database that I can recall in order to uplift myself when I'm in an emotionally bad place. There is always something, no matter how small, that we can put in our own mental database and use when we need a little boost. In this case, mine was that I *could* stand up to bullies. Bullies like easy targets, and when someone stands up to them, they often back off. I don't need to be an easy target.

More recently, I worked at an IT service provider startup. The company had established a strong reputation for modernizing technology and transitioning it to the cloud. The group of engineers there who were responsible for crafting tailor-made solutions for clients were highly revered, resulting in some developing huge egos. This one engineer was particularly arrogant and condescending, frequently flaunting his accomplishments and knowledge to assert his superiority. His disrespect extended to those outside the technology-related departments, like the folks in human resources, finance, and procurement.

In one fateful meeting, this engineer rudely interrupted me while I was suggesting a solution to a particular problem. He condescendingly said, "Since you are only good at buying paper and pencils, you wouldn't understand what we are trying to do here." He then proceeded to tear down my suggestion and idea. His words were not only unexpected but deeply hurtful. I maintained my composure, concealing my embarrassment and anger. Not seeing the reaction he was hoping for, he repeated his insult again, this time louder and more emphatic. I maintained my composure, and the meeting continued without further incident.

Although I pride myself on possessing emotional resilience in the workplace (after all, I had lots of practice earlier in my childhood), I am not immune to hurt feelings. I do bleed when cut. On that particular day, for whatever reason, his comments deeply wounded me. On the drive back home, I couldn't shake his words from my mind; they echoed continuously, causing me to tear up. What infuriated me was that when he didn't see the reaction from me that he wanted to see, he repeated the insult again, essentially plunging the knife deeper into me while twisting it to ensure he left a lasting mark. After a few deep breaths, I reminded myself that I was much more than what he said I was or perceived me to be. I don't purchase office supplies, and never have, as a profession. In my previous role, I had managed a staggering $2.2 billion in company spending, with my team purchasing infrastructure equipment, software, and services. This perspective shift allowed me to regain my sense of confidence and pivot away from the negative emotional response I found myself spiraling into. Asking the question, *Is the thing this person said about me true?* can help tremendously. In my case, the answer was an unequivocal *no*.

If what someone says about us is not true, we know we don't have to pay any attention to it or waste any of our emotional energy on it.

Understanding the insignificance of untrue criticisms about us underscores the power of a perspective shift. By recognizing that these unfounded opinions do not reflect our true selves, we empower ourselves to rise above the noise and focus on what truly matters—our own perception and self-worth. It took me a while to get to this place. This mental realignment not only conserves our emotional energy but also redirects it toward more constructive and self-affirming endeavors. Embracing this shift in perspective transforms how we respond to negativity, turning potential stumbling blocks into stepping stones for personal growth and resilience. It teaches us that our energy is precious and should be invested in thoughts and actions that nurture our well-being and authentic selves, rather than being drained by baseless judgments.

Sometimes, when you are seen as a great and valuable member of the team at work, the level at which you do that great work is the level where your management wants to keep you. I remember one of my managers in the past commenting that I did great work and that he would like to keep me in the "basement" cranking out that work so no one would be the wiser about his "secret weapon." He meant this as a compliment, but what his comments told me was that management did not see me as being capable of becoming a true leader that could be seen! Just a basement worker bee at best. Not good. Time to move on.

As a woman in this competitive environment, I quickly saw the truth in the adage that women must work twice as hard for recognition. My female colleagues and I found ourselves having to explain more and work harder and longer hours to prove our worth. A study conducted by Lean In and McKinsey & Company found that "For every 100 men promoted to manager, only 85 women were promoted," indicating that women are less likely to receive their first promotion into management than men, despite asking for promotions at similar rates.[8] This realization didn't embitter me; instead, it motivated me to focus and strive harder, without harboring any hard feelings. This is key for me, and it frees me up to focus my energy on doing my best rather than spiraling downward in resentment.

Another reason I worked harder than most was because I was the only one taking care of my children, so staying employed was always top of mind for me. Not an ideal situation! There needs to be a balance. I was so consumed with the need to be financially secure for us as a family that I lost sight of striking a good balance. To this day, I feel very guilty about spending so much more time working than with the kids when they were growing up. Back then, I was shocked to hear that a colleague, who was also a single mom, quit her job without a backup plan. It was a reminder of the delicate tightrope I was walking. When I asked her how she was going to take care of her children, she casually said, "The government will take care of us." Such decisions, while shocking, also highlight the diverse and often desperate strategies single parents employ to survive.

If you will recall, I love to learn, and my corporate life was filled with so many opportunities to do so—courses ranging from improving specific technical skills to general management and leadership seminars and programs. I soaked up all these teachings, and I took what I learned and continuously put it into practice. I also enrolled myself in college classes while working full-time and graduated with a degree in finance. My father was not able to afford to send me to college earlier in my life, so at the first opportunity, I sent myself and earned my degree. Not being able to attend college at age eighteen does not mean one can't pursue it at age twenty-eight, thirty-eight, forty-eight, or beyond. In our digital world, educational pursuits are available globally and can be accessed easily. Online courses cover a wide range of disciplines and topics, from computer science and health to business and the humanities, sometimes at a fraction of the cost of regular tuition. One can learn from world-class faculty while joining a global community of learners. It is up to each individual to want it enough to first see it and then be brave enough to go for it! There is always a way.

When interacting with male colleagues or business associates, it's crucial to be mindful of how our behaviors and signals might be interpreted. Sometimes, actions or words meant to be friendly and professional can be misconstrued as indications of romantic interest. This misunderstanding can lead to unwanted advances, creating situations that are not only awkward but potentially traumatic. My own experience in this arena taught me just how important it is to maintain clear boundaries and be aware of the messages I may be unintentionally sending when interacting with male colleagues, business associates, and even friends. By just being aware of the potential misconceptions, we can help ensure that our professional interactions remain respectful and appropriate.

The positive professional achievements, as well as the negative experiences in my life thus far, seemed to be like a whirlwind that zipped me forward at warp speed. Amid it all, a serendipitous twist of fate was quietly unfolding, leading me toward a new horizon. Unbeknownst to me, I stood at the threshold of a deeply personal adventure—a heartwarming tale of companionship, love, and new beginnings.

CHAPTER 9

A New Chapter

MY JOURNEY TO THE US was not just a geographical move; it was a journey from a past filled with shadows into a new world of possibilities, including leaving an abusive relationship. One of the most unanticipated aspects of this move was meeting Alan, a fellow banker with a charming smile and warm demeanor. Alan's interest in me was clear from the start. All he knew about me was that I worked at the international division of a bank in downtown Dallas. He went out of his way to find out more about me, even asking around to get my contact information. When he finally called, inviting me for lunch, I was hesitant. I couldn't even remember what he looked like, and I turned down his offer, laughing it off as a case of mistaken identity.

But Alan was persistent. After several failed attempts to get me to go out for a meal with him, he offered to take all the women in my department out to lunch with us if I was nervous about going out with him alone. I felt bad and accepted his invitation, and I arranged to meet him for lunch at the deli located in my office building. When I told him about my children, half expecting him to lose interest, he surprised me. Not only did he not run away, he seemed more intrigued. Our conversations grew longer, our meetings more frequent, and before I knew it, we were dating. After a year, our relationship progressed to a point where the possibility of forming a family with Alan and his parents became more real. However, my first encounter with them was less than heartwarming.

We decided to take them to a buffet at one of their favorite restaurants—a gesture to show my eagerness to get to know them and be part of the family. The evening started well enough, with conversation flowing easily. But I soon noticed a troubling pattern. Whenever Alan left our table to get more food, his parents would clam up and become distant and cold. At first, I thought it was the noise of the restaurant drowning out my voice, so I spoke louder. But it became painfully clear that they were deliberately ignoring me, their eyes fixed on their plates, refusing to engage until Alan returned. This was my first startling realization of their disapproval, a silent yet eloquent expression of their feelings toward me. Our encounters from there were few and far between. My efforts to connect with this family were met with blank stares or polite nods and short one- or two-word responses, depending on who was around to witness these exchanges.

As our wedding day approached, my excitement was tinged with apprehension due to those several cold receptions at family gatherings, as well as the initial one. My mother and sister flew in from Singapore to share in what was meant to be a joyful occasion. Alan's parents were also in town for the wedding. In an attempt to try to get Alan's parents to engage in conversations with us, my mom, my sister, and I decided to prepare a big American breakfast for them. It was our way of providing an opportunity for all of us to get to know each other over a good meal. We woke up early, cooking sausages, eggs, bacon, and toast, and set the table with care.

But as the minutes ticked by, there was no sign of them. Our gentle knocks on their bedroom door went unanswered. They chose to stay in their room, ignoring our efforts. This was more than just a rejection of a meal; it was a clear message of their unwillingness to accept us. I felt a pang of disappointment, a heavy feeling in my heart as I realized this was yet another sign of their disapproval. With a heavy heart and a sense of duty, I called Alan to inform him of the situation. Following his advice, we ate quietly, made sure we left enough food for them, and left for my final dress fitting. Apparently, they did come out after we departed and ate up the food we had left for them.

The evening before the wedding day, we were all heading out to dinner, and Alan's mother caused a ruckus, saying that she was feeling ill, and refused to go. She insisted on staying behind and was especially upset when even her husband encouraged her to join everyone on this happy occasion. Although we all proceeded with our plan and went on, this put a damper on the evening for all of us. Another unnecessary drama intended to cause disruption.

The wedding day arrived, buzzing with energy and excitement. Friends from diverse backgrounds—Asians, Caucasians, African Americans, Indians, and Iranians—filled our home, each person contributing to the joyous occasion. However, Alan's parents' behavior cast a shadow over the festivities. They interacted only with Caucasian guests, Alan's best man, who is African American, and a childhood friend they knew. Their blatant avoidance of our other friends was painfully obvious.

The situation became particularly awkward when my Iranian friend, who was kindly doing my nails, offered to do the same for Alan's mother. The offer was met with a cold stare and utter silence, an uncomfortable moment that left everyone around feeling uneasy. I quickly distracted my friend, and we went on discussing her children's soccer activities.

At the wedding reception, Alan's parents' disapproval was more evident than ever. They stood aloof, refusing to interact with any of the other guests. When spoken to, they simply nodded. Their behavior was so noticeable that several of my colleagues from the bank expressed their sympathy over the situation. I couldn't help but think that their presence, so full of disapproval, did more harm than good. It would have been better if they had chosen not to attend, like Alan's brother and sisters. Even the photographer, while taking group pictures, had to ask them both to smile as "this is a happy occasion." Their intention to make their stance clear to every one of our friends was painfully successful.

With our honeymoon scheduled for the next day, Alan, having seen how his parents had treated my mom and sister, was worried about how they would treat them in his absence. He decided to address the issue head-on, suggesting to his parents that it might be best for everyone if they left first thing the next day. This suggestion did not go over well. The next day, everyone seemed to be on their best behavior when we left on our honeymoon. But a few hours after we left the house, Alan's best man called to tell Alan his mom was on a rampage. She went around the house dramatically tearing down all the curtains in every room, saying they were hers because she had made them. Then she took some other small items from the house, claiming she had bought them for Alan, and left in a huff and a puff. The story told to the rest of his family was that Alan had, with my encouragement, thrown them out of his house. I only found out what Alan had told them after that phone call from his best man. Alan knew if he had told me before he acted, I would have stopped him.

The events surrounding our wedding were a whirlwind of emotions—joy, excitement, frustration, disappointment, and sadness. They tested our resilience as a couple and marked the beginning of our journey together, a journey that was already proving to be as challenging as it was beautiful.

In the years that followed our wedding, Alan and I settled into the rhythm of family life—juggling work, the kids' activities, and the everyday demands of running a household and global travel for both of us. Life, with its busy routine, seemed to march on. Alan occasionally reached out to his mother, attempting to bridge the gap that had formed, and was happy to find their conversations were always pleasant. His mom never gave any hint that she was upset or still harboring resentment.

Five years into our marriage, we moved into a bigger home, a milestone that filled us with a sense of excitement and possibility. With Thanksgiving approaching, the new guest room presented an opportunity for me to suggest to Alan that we extend an invitation to his unmarried sister to spend the holiday with us. He agreed, thinking it was a wonderful idea.

Our spirits were high as we dialed her number, eager to enjoy this moment and create new memories. But the moment she answered, our optimism was met with a cold, unfamiliar tone. "Who is this?" she asked. When Alan identified himself as her brother, there was a palpable pause and a moment of disbelief. Her next words struck us like a bolt of lightning. "Oh, you didn't know? Until you leave that bitch, you are no longer a member of our family."

We stood there, phone in hand, speechless and stunned. Our balloon of hope was not just deflated, it was burst with a very loud pop! As Alan started to rebuke her for her harsh words, I intervened, pointing out that the pain her words inflicted was not toward me since I hardly knew her. The person she was really hurting was her own brother. Her response was a scream laden with anger and hate: "Shut up, you bitch!" At that moment, Alan and I realized the futility of our efforts. We hung up, a silent understanding passing between us. Wow, I couldn't understand how anyone could hate a person they hardly knew. We were crushed.

This painful encounter was a revelation for Alan. It shed light on why he had not heard from his siblings all these years, and why his parents only spoke to him when he called them. There was not a single hint in his conversations with his mother that there was anything wrong or that his family had disowned him. On reflection, it should not have surprised him. In his family, issues were swept under the rug, problems were left unaddressed, and a facade of normalcy was maintained. This was their way of dealing with problems—by pretending they didn't exist. The curses Alan's sister hurled at me were meant to hurt me, but frankly, they just bounced off me.

All those years, although I tried to connect with them, they didn't make any effort to get to know me. From my perspective, they were no different than strangers I met on the street. I am respectful and kind to everyone I meet, and I afforded them the same courtesies. We only feel hurt when people we care about treat us unfairly. There was no relationship between me and Alan's family, and anything they said would be like the man in the truck at the mall who told me to go back to my own country. Ok . . . maybe a bit worse, since they are Alan's family and I do wish we had a good relationship. So it did hurt a little that they had rejected me.

The aftermath of the failed Thanksgiving invitation took an unexpected turn when Alan later learned from his father about the twisted narrative his sister had spun. She had told the rest of the family that it was me who had called and hurled insults at her over the phone. What was intended as a gesture of goodwill had been contorted into an ugly falsehood. This marked the last time Alan spoke to this sister, a painful severing of ties over a misrepresentation. I was surprised, and still am today, that no one questioned why I would do such a thing out of the blue, after so many years. When we are so consumed by our emotions (good or bad), we are often blind to everything else, and our minds close to other possibilities.

Sometime later, Alan received a call from his parents, who were in town and wanted to meet him for lunch. I was at work, so Alan went alone, hoping to finally understand the root of their disapproval of me. During lunch, he candidly asked his parents why they were so adamantly against our marriage. His parents had never really taken the time to get to know me, yet they seemed so certain that he had made a grave mistake, and the hatred they had for me was puzzling.

The answer came from his father, who bluntly stated that he and his wife believed I had married Alan for his money. What money? Alan was astounded. He had grown up in poverty and was a self-made software engineer when we met. He put himself through school, working two jobs with no help from his parents. As mentioned earlier, in chapter 8, I too put myself through school when I came to the US while working full-time. We were both hardworking corporate professionals, far from the image of wealth that could attract a gold digger. If anything, my family could easily accuse Alan of marrying me for my family's money (not mine). The absurdity of their belief was almost laughable, a clear indication of how misconceptions can fuel unwarranted animosity. Their view of the world was so narrow and small that they thought because I am not from the United States, I must come from an underdeveloped country where we live in huts and sleep on dirt-packed floors, so even an average working-class American would appear to be a gold mine I could latch myself onto and benefit from!

Nevertheless, the truth was out, even if they were misinformed and mistaken. It provided me with a level of closure, and I was not left wondering anymore. The lesson here is that when we want to know the truth and ask, we must be prepared for the answer to not be what we were expecting, fair, or even well represented.

If my in-laws had been more open-minded or stayed current on world news, they would have known that Singapore is renowned for its robust economy and high standard of living. As one of the world's leading financial centers, it has a significant number of wealthy individuals, including millionaires. Singapore's gross domestic product (GDP) per capita has been shown to be among the highest globally, indicating the country's wealth and economic prosperity. The Republic's GDP growth for 2024 was projected at 2.4 percent, up from 2023 results.[9]

Singapore also consistently ranks high in terms of the ratio of millionaires to the general population. According to Credit Suisse's 2023 Global Wealth Report, Singapore ranked tenth in the world for mean wealth per adult, and while specific numbers can fluctuate yearly due to economic changes and wealth growth, it was also reported that one-third of the adult population in Singapore falls into this category of millionaires in US dollar terms.[10] This high concentration reflects Singapore's successful economic policies, its role as a global financial hub, and its attractiveness to wealthy individuals and investors worldwide. It goes to show that ignorance is not always bliss, and it can even be dangerous.

Later that day, after Alan returned to work, I received a distressing call from our children. Alan's parents had shown up at our home, demanding entry to their son's house. Out of fear, our daughter opened the door. They barged in, took pictures of every room, and left as abruptly as they had arrived. The reason for their visit later became clear to us—they wanted to see the house we had bought. All they had to do was ask, and we would have given them a *legitimate* tour of the house. I felt a deep sense of violation, and I told Alan half-jokingly that next time, I'd draw a line down the middle of the house and restrict them to their son's half of the house. But beneath the joke was a real sense of intrusion and disrespect. How rude!

In light of these incidents, Alan and I made a conscious decision to rise above their rude, immature, and ignorant behavior—chalking it up to their lack of social graces. We vowed to maintain our integrity, refusing to stoop to retaliation or pettiness. It was a choice to move forward with grace, despite the unjust treatment. Many of my colleagues expressed their respect for my patience with my in-laws, as I still treated them kindly in the handful of times we've met in all these years. They said they would have given up a long time ago. I believe we each have a set of core values that we live by, and no matter how we are being treated, we need to remind ourselves of those values and not waver or respond in ways that are contrary to them.

It's unfortunate that Alan's parents chose to behave this way. With my own family far away on the other side of the world, I was so looking forward to having a family (Alan's) here in the US. I was more than willing to welcome them into our lives and even have them stay with us occasionally or join us on vacations. Life could have been so much more enjoyable for them without their baseless complaints and unwarranted animosity toward me. For example, at that time, we would go to Colorado for downhill skiing every other year and always had a blast. They could have joined us. I wouldn't have expected them to ski, but while we were out on the slopes, they could have been sitting in the restaurant up in the mountains looking down at the beautiful scenery while having a hot cup of cocoa, walking around the quaint little shops in the villages below, or sitting in the hot tub at the condo. There were other vacations in the US (Disney World, beaches, etc.) and in many parts of Europe as well. It's rather sad to think about, and such a missed opportunity; we would have loved to spend time with family while, at the same time, experiencing other cultures around the world!

By then, I was a busy executive, with neither the time nor the patience for such needless drama. Alan and I decided we had tried our best to foster a good relationship with them, but now the ball was in their court. We would be there when they decided to reengage with us. Our focus was on forging our own family unit and establishing our legacy for our children. We are blessed that both our daughter and son grew up to be well-adjusted, responsible, and well-mannered adults.

The essence of my story lies in the recognition of one's self-worth. Understanding that your worth is not contingent on external validation, but rather something inherent and unique to you is liberating. As I navigated through the waves of change and embraced new chapters in my life, this understanding of self-worth became my guiding light, illuminating paths I never thought I'd travel. I consciously and intentionally put aside such discrimination from Alan's family, knowing their opinions of me do not equal who I am.

CHAPTER 10

I Am Not Ugly After All

MOVING TO THE US opened a new chapter in my life, one filled with unexpected realizations and heartwarming surprises. Back in Singapore when growing up, as I shared earlier, the shadows of being labeled the ugly one due to my darker complexion lingered in my mind. But here, in this new country, I encountered a series of amusing and surprising moments that challenged this deep-seated belief.

It started with my colleagues at work. I was taken aback when a few of them expressed their interest in me, extending invitations for coffee or lunch. This was new and, quite frankly, a bit overwhelming. I just thought that they were being polite and nice. Then, there were the bus drivers and passengers at the park and ride who greeted me with warm smiles and sometimes struck up conversations, with some even mustering the courage to ask me out.

But it didn't stop there. After a minor auto accident where my car spun around and around on the slick highway after an ice storm, eventually hitting a semitruck, the policeman who came to the scene was more interested in knowing if I was single than the details of the incident. And then there were those random strangers at the bus stop and on the bus who would sometimes compliment me or strike up a conversation that hinted at more than just passing the time.

For the first time, I looked in the mirror and thought, *Maybe I'm not that ugly after all*. This realization was empowering. It was as if I had been viewing myself through a distorted lens all this time, and now, that lens was slowly being corrected.

Amid this newfound realization, I wasn't actively seeking love; my focus and top priority was on adjusting to my new life and taking care of my children. I had zero interest in dating or anything related to it. However, as often happens, love found me when I least expected it. That was when I met Alan, as narrated in the previous chapter.

As my journey unfolded, I discovered that our self-perception is often a collage of the opinions and judgments we've collected from others over the years. In my case, moving to a new environment, away from the labels and biases of my past, allowed me to see myself in a new light. It taught me an important lesson—the image we hold of ourselves is not set in stone; it can change, evolve, and even be completely rewritten in new contexts.

This experience also highlighted the unexpected nature of love. It's often said that love finds us when we least expect it, and my story was a testament to that. In my life, focused on adjusting to a new country and caring for my children, love was the last thing on my mind. Yet, it was during this period of unintentional solitude that love gently made its presence known. It reminded me that life has a way of surprising us with beautiful moments, especially when we're open and able to trust that life happens for us and not to us.

I also learned the importance of overcoming past beliefs, particularly those about oneself. Shedding the long-held belief that I was ugly was not just a moment of revelation; it was a step toward embracing my worth and realizing that I was more than the labels I had grown up with. So what if I am not as beautiful and fair in complexion as the women I see on magazine covers? This transformation was not just about how others saw me but, more importantly, how I saw myself.

Navigating through years of trauma and finding moments of joy amid adversity required more than just a hopeful mindset; it demanded focused, intentional actions. A mindset geared toward recovery and resilience is crucial, but without concrete steps, it remains merely aspirational. In the next chapter, I will share the framework that I consistently used to guide me in taking the intentional steps to break free from the limiting beliefs that have held me back.

Throughout all these challenges, my guiding light was the purpose I set for myself and my children—to escape the past's shadows and provide them with opportunities I never had. My children's well-being is my North Star, and focusing on that has helped me navigate the complexities of life—not just in a foreign land but life as a whole.

My approach to my career in corporate America was rooted in a simple yet powerful philosophy: do the best job possible and help others achieve their goals. This belief came from the inspired quote from Zig Ziglar, "You can have everything in life you want, if you will just help enough other people get what they want."[11] Zig Ziglar, a wise, kind, funny, and wonderful man, was my Sunday school teacher for a few years when I lived in Plano, Texas. I clung on to his sound advice and many other teachings and put them into practice. My belief in helping others succeed was recognized and rewarded by my employers, leading to significant advancements. I am grateful to Zig for teaching me.

My mindset has been my most powerful tool. Having, and intentionally setting, the right mindset has helped me to move forward by focusing on what is the best course for me without being distracted by blaming, wallowing in the past, or being stuck in inaction. Resilience and grit became my core values. Here are some mantras that I've used over the years:

- *I can figure this out.* As far back as I can remember, I've always believed this to be true to the core of my being. I'm not sure where it came from, but it is one of my superpowers. As Henry Ford said, "Whether you think you can, or you think you can't—you're right."[12] Because I believe I can figure things out, I almost always do. Not always eloquently, but hey, whatever works!
- *This too shall pass.* Tough times would pass, and I had the strength to overcome any hurdle. My faith was a cornerstone of this resilience, encapsulated in the verse from Philippians 4:13: "I can do all things through Christ who strengthens me," a phrase that I have carried with me on a worn-out card for over forty years.[13] I pull this card out to read it whenever I need uplifting, and especially did so when I was bullied, marginalized, discounted, and unkindly judged in the workplace.
- *Hang in there; don't give up too easily. Try one more time.* Sometimes, I embellish this and say, *You are not a person who gives up easily.*

In each of these mantras, I found strength and solace. Whether it was persevering through another challenging day at work, navigating the complexities of life in a new country, or standing strong against personal violations, these affirmations were my beacon of hope and strength. My wish is that you will find them to be helpful for you too.

Embracing change is another powerful mindset tool. Sometimes, a radical change, like relocating, can be a path to healing and growth. This mindset is about stepping out of comfort zones and embracing new opportunities, even in the face of uncertainty. It doesn't have to be as drastic as, such as in my case, escaping to another country; it can be as simple as a change in your current environment or how you engage with others by setting boundaries. It's said that people don't like change, and there is a lot of truth in that. People will go to great lengths to avoid change both at home and in the workplace. Just ask the change management gurus in any field; they will have loads of stories to share. In order for us to thrive, we need to tune and condition our minds to believe change is just an opportunity for growth.

I hope my insights can inspire and comfort you, my readers, who may face similar situations.

In my pursuit of healing, I challenged myself to revisit my past and not dwell in fear and hatred. I viewed the hardships my father faced not as excuses but as explanations that paint a fuller picture of his challenges and help reveal different aspects of my father I had not considered. This endeavor was not about excusing his actions (he was wrong to be physically abusive) but about understanding the complexity of human relationships and emotions.

Recognizing his struggles helped me to humanize him, softening the sharp edges of my memories. I realized it must have been difficult for him to be yanked from the comfort of his home and family and whisked away to a foreign country to live with strangers when he was still a teenager. He had to forge his way on his own with no guidance or even good role models. It couldn't have been easy for him, with no formal higher education, to forge a living that would support two wives and seven children who were totally dependent on him. At one point, I know he made $500 a month. To this day, I am not sure how he made it all work. My mom would help by sewing clothes for nearby factories. Growing up, I did not feel we were poor or deprived in any way. They did a good job providing for us.

I also realized that empathy could coexist with the pain caused by my father's actions. This duality did not diminish the hurt, but it offered a path toward a more nuanced understanding of my father's character. As I pieced together these fragments of his life, I found myself reconciling with parts of my own story that I had struggled to accept. This process of reflection and understanding emphasized the transformative power of empathy—not only in healing old wounds but preventing new ones. It reminded me that everyone carries their history into their actions, and while this doesn't excuse hurtful behavior, it can inform a deeper, more compassionate response.

As I looked back, I discovered instances that indicated my father's love for us, his children. Though he never verbally expressed his affection, his actions, at times, spoke volumes. Whether it was his dedication to providing for the family, his efforts to protect us in his own way, or the subtle ways he tried to connect with us, it became evident that there was more to him than the narrative of abuse had allowed me to see. As most people with kids know, our children don't come with instruction manuals. Parents often do the best they can with what they know and have at that time.

He was the one who taught us all our table manners—from waiting till everyone is seated at the table before starting to eat to no elbows on the table and not speaking with your mouths full all the way to how to properly eat peas with a fork and knife (nope, not stabbing or scooping the peas with your fork). We were cautious not to say within his earshot that we loved to eat something because the next thing we knew, he would buy a ton of what we liked and make us eat it until we became sick of that food. His reasoning? He didn't want us to grow up and be easily enticed by ill-meaning men with things we crave! Right or wrong, his intentions there were meant for good.

The lessons we learned translate into other areas, not just food. A good example is when I had been living here in the US for barely a year, a much older and rich bank customer invited me to go to Cancun with him. I didn't know where Cancun was, so he described it as heaven on earth. He further assured me that he would take care of everything and that I would not have to pay a dime for this trip. I was not attracted to his offer because I remembered the lesson that my father had drummed into me and understood that I would be paying for this trip, just not with money!

He also gave me career advice. When I rose quickly in the corporate world, I found myself bragging to my father one day about how nice people were to me. He warned me that because of my position in the company, some people may be nice to the chair I sit on and not to me personally, and if that was the case, to not be disappointed when I found those same people not to be so nice when I moved on and vacated that chair. Their loyalties would shift quickly to the next person who occupies that chair. That, he said, is part of corporate life. The ones that stick with you regardless of the position you hold will be the ones you can trust and form long-term relationships with. Great advice!

My father also made us wear leather shoes growing up. They were stiff and uncomfortable, and we hated them. Our schoolmates wore tennis shoes, and we wanted those instead but would not dare to ask for them. His reasoning? Hard leather shoes would shape our feet nicely as we grew up. Another so-called beauty tip he gave me when I was in my twenties was to remember that the first sign of aging in a woman is in her hands and to take care of my hands as well as I take care of the skin on my face. I believed him even back then because I knew he was an expert when it came to women, and since that day, whatever I put on my face I also apply to my hands!

On a more serious note, when I was in Texas, my father had heard that—unlike in Singapore, a city on an island where everyone can walk to places—no one walks anywhere in Texas. Everything is spread out, and the weather in the summer is too hot to walk. He sent me the cash to purchase a car. Knowing I would not accept it because I knew he didn't have much himself, he came up with a story that he had won a small lottery and wanted to share his good fortune with all his children. Having a car made my life much easier.

I remember once when I was about ten, after an especially brutal beating from my father, my mom walked out of the house. I sat on the porch, waiting all day for her to come home. My father came to the door a couple of times and saw that I had not moved from my spot. Then he left the house to go look for my mom. For a very proud man to put aside his ego to go looking for his wife because he saw his daughter hurting and waiting for her mom to come home showed the tremendous love he had for me. I learned later from my mom that she had intended to end her life that day. However, when she was about to do it, my father's best friend (who had died a few years prior) appeared and comforted her. In the end, this friend told her to go home to her kids. I can't tell if my mom actually saw or imagined this good friend, but she felt comforted by him and decided to return home. My father never found her, but looking back, I know it took a lot of courage and love for him to put aside his humongous ego to go looking for a wife, not because he cared whether she lived or died, but because he saw I was hurting and missing my mom.

One of the biggest surprises we had was when my sister invited my parents to a church service and even my father went. The surprise was not his attendance but that, when the preacher made the invitation, my father went up to accept Christ as his Savior! That shocked all of us. His reasoning? He went up there so my sister would not be embarrassed (in his words, "lose face") at her church. My father was a very devoted Taoist, and for him to walk down that aisle because he was thinking more of my sister than himself spoke volumes of his love for her!

There are many more instances when I saw my father's love for me shine through. I was just too blinded by fear and anger to see them back then. When Alan and I got engaged, Alan called my father to introduce himself and asked for his blessing to marry me. They had a short (because of the limits of my father's English) but good conversation, and before they ended the call, my father told Alan that he could now "die in peace," as he knew that I was being taken care of.

I love my dad!

CHAPTER 11

Empowerment Through Adversity—The Iron Will Framework

EMBARKING ON A JOURNEY to overcome the shadows of adversity and trauma requires courage, perseverance, and an ironclad will to forge ahead. In this chapter, I share strategies and the framework that has been my compass and anchor through the stormiest seas of my past. Each step, born from personal and professional trials and triumphs, is designed to guide you beyond the chains of limiting beliefs that have held you captive and toward a horizon of strength, self-discovery, and empowerment. This framework is more than a collection of steps; it's a blueprint for breaking free from the confines of your past and embracing the boundless potential of your future. Welcome to your journey of transformation, where every step taken is a step toward the liberation of your true self.

Break the Silence

The first step is breaking the silence. Don't keep your pain a secret out of shame or fear of being judged. There is power in voicing personal and professional struggles. Here is how you might expand and enhance this step:

Personal

Journaling as an initial safe space is an excellent start. I started by journaling, and I dumped all my feelings on paper where no one could see them. In this space, I felt safe and could express all my emotions freely. Writing these thoughts and feelings down after years of keeping them bottled up inside was very freeing and therapeutic for me. To build on this, consider incorporating structured reflection prompts that can guide you to deeper introspection, such as the following:

- What am I feeling (sad, angry, afraid, etc.) and why?
- What strengths have helped me to endure in the past?
- Why am I afraid to share my story?

This structured approach can prepare you for discussing your experiences more openly with others. Once I started feeling better, I shared snippets of my story with my spouse and one trusted friend. Opening up about my past to others can be liberating, and it helps me feel less alone. Additionally, engaging in support groups where shared experiences foster a sense of community can further diminish feelings of isolation.

Professional

I suffered in silence when bullied at work (especially when it came from one of my bosses) out of fear of retribution and shame in having to admit that I was too intimidated to stand up for myself. Beyond confronting workplace bullying, it's crucial to develop a strategy for reporting such incidents. Documenting specific instances, seeking allies within the organization, and understanding your company's policies on harassment are practical steps. Also, consider professional counseling or coaching tailored to assertiveness training or conflict resolution to strengthen your personal advocacy skills in the workplace.

Breaking free from the burden of silence is a courageous step toward reclaiming your life and well-being. You are not alone, and there is help and support available to guide you on the path to healing and safety.

For companies looking to give their employees a sense of safety, creating something I like to call a "silence breaker's toolkit" could be valuable. This toolkit might include resources like contact information for therapists, guidelines for navigating HR channels, tips for effective journaling, and ways to cultivate resilience. Sharing such tools not only equips employees to take their first step toward healing and recovery but also shows them that management cares about their well-being and that bad behaviors are not tolerated under their watch.

Be Open to Receive

I had closed myself up pretty tightly for years. I've always given a lot of myself and have not hesitated to help others. But I eventually realized that I didn't really know how to receive help, or maybe even love and support. I think this came from a fear of trusting someone and then getting hurt again. However, the baby steps I took in sharing tidbits of my story did help me begin to see the support and acceptance offered by others. I started to tell myself to remain open and willing to receive help from others. This little switch in my mindset opened my eyes to see outside of my little, dark world (my mind). There are many, many good, supportive, and loving people out there if we just allow ourselves to see them.

Personal

Engage in self-reflection exercises that help you explore your own barriers to receiving. Asking yourself questions like those below can open you up to deeper understanding and acceptance of help:

- What am I afraid of?
- What does receiving mean to me?

Incorporate a daily gratitude practice where you acknowledge one thing you received each day, whether it's a compliment, help from a colleague, or a kind gesture from a stranger. This can gradually change the perception that receiving is a sign of weakness to a celebration of interconnectedness.

Professional

Being open to receiving can translate into seeking mentorship and guidance. Reach out to mentors within your industry who can open doors to new opportunities and enhance your professional growth.

Sometimes we shrink back from fully engaging at work for fear of being criticized. It is important that we shift our outlook or perception of criticisms into constructive feedback, not as something meant to hurt but as a gift aimed at one's professional and personal growth. I found this shift in mindset helped me to be less anxious and more willing to engage fully.

To assist with this mindset shift, I use visualization techniques to imagine scenarios where accepting help leads to positive outcomes. This not only helped me with my anxieties about being judged or criticized but also reduced the fear I associated with vulnerability.

Give yourself a monthly challenge to pick an area where you usually wouldn't ask for help and step out there to do it. This can be anything from asking for advice on a personal project to seeking professional guidance on career advancements.

Embrace Patience

The journey to recovery and self-discovery is neither swift nor direct. As with many other worthwhile endeavors, it takes time. I constantly remind myself to be patient, understanding that progress involves a mix of forward strides and inevitable setbacks. Acknowledging this from the start helps temper my expectations, preventing discouragement at the first sign of a stumble. It is not going to be a straight or linear path to the other side. It took me a few decades to figure out my purpose. Trying out some of the tips I have offered in this book should help you take less time. Have faith; it will come.

Personal

Practicing mindfulness techniques like deep-breathing exercises or guided meditations can help calm the mind, making it easier to accept the pace of progress. There are many free videos online that you can try in order to see what works for you. Additionally, try keeping a patience journal where you can note moments you felt impatient and how you addressed these feelings. Reflecting back on these entries can provide insights into personal growth or even the effectiveness of writing them down. If you are already journaling, add a note or two about your wins in being patient that day.

Professional

Setting long-term goals is helpful, as patience is required to achieve them. This can be particularly relevant when career advancements or significant projects take time to come to fruition. In the meantime, celebrating the small wins along the way not only helps reinforce patience but also keeps motivation levels high.

The connection between patience and resilience is profound because both are essential in navigating life's challenges. Patience allows individuals to endure difficult circumstances without frustration or despair, which is crucial when progress seems slow or obscured. This ability to withstand trials fosters resilience, reinforcing our capacity to recover from setbacks. Resilient people often view challenges as opportunities for growth, and this perspective is strengthened by the patience to persevere through the process of overcoming obstacles. Thus, cultivating patience not only helps us to manage immediate difficulties but also builds the resilience needed for long-term success and stability.

Set a Routine

Navigating single parenthood without financial support or a robust support network can feel like steering a ship through stormy seas. Despite the many challenges, creating a stable environment for yourself and your children (if you have any) while remaining flexible to adjust and adapt to unexpected changes will help to provide a modicum of peace and allow you to maintain focus amid chaos.

When I was trying to get settled in my life as a single mom, living in a foreign country, and working a full-time career outside the home, I found setting a routine provided a sense of stability and security. Whenever I feel the chaos and responsibilities getting to me, even to this day, I focus on just following whatever's next on my schedule. That's it. Very soon, I found myself moving calmly, step by step, through my day, just following the routine schedule I had set for myself and the children. This also created a stable environment for the children.

Maintaining a routine also offers predictability, which is crucial for children, especially in a single-parent household. Knowing what to expect each day helps reduce anxiety and build confidence in children. For the parent, sticking to a schedule helps segment overwhelming responsibilities into manageable tasks, making them feel more achievable and less daunting.

Personal

In the morning chaos of trying to get the children ready for school and yourself ready for work, there is little or no time to spare for anything else. However, setting a morning ritual of even just a few minutes to center yourself by taking ten deep breaths can set a positive tone for the rest of your day. If possible, wake up half an hour earlier to do some self-care.

Designating specific times for meals or activities with children can reinforce a sense of security and togetherness, which is crucial for single and busy parents navigating challenges.

Professional

To effectively get more work done, try time-blocking to manage your tasks at work. Managing a heavy workload while I was writing this book was undoubtedly challenging, especially since I was also committed to maintaining my blog (*https://wendycwilson.com*) by adding new posts twice a month.

Time-blocking became my go-to strategy to get everything done. By allocating specific blocks of time to different tasks, I created a structured schedule that allowed me to focus intensely on one task at a time without feeling overwhelmed. For example, I designated certain hours of the day ahead of time for solely writing my book and other hours of my day for planning and drafting blog posts. During these dedicated time blocks, I turned off phone notifications and minimized distractions, creating a focused environment where I could immerse myself fully in the task at hand. The effectiveness of time-blocking lies in its ability to provide a clear roadmap for the day, reducing the anxiety of juggling multiple responsibilities. By breaking down my workload into manageable chunks and assigning them to specific times, I found a balance that kept me productive and prevented burnout. This method is especially helpful when one is feeling overwhelmed, and it can also increase your productivity.

Taking scheduled breaks to avoid burnout is also important. Even a few minutes of closing your eyes every hour or two can help. If time allows, take a short five- to ten-minute walk to clear the mind and help boost energy.

Prioritize Self-Care and Self-Love

Taking care of ourselves is usually the first thing that we neglect when going through major change or traumatic times in our lives. Remembering to take time to check in on our emotional state of mind is important. Engage in activities that bring you joy and enable you to surround yourself with people who uplift and support you.

In my quest to take better care of myself, I block off some time each day in my calendar for just me. During this me-time,

I do different things I enjoy; for example, I work out, sit in a sauna, meditate, journal, study self-development, or read. What would your me-time look like? Even taking a fifteen-minute break to meditate, reflect, or just get a cup of coffee or tea can make a difference. Prioritizing self-care and self-love is essential, and that means being intentional in doing so. When my schedule during the day is packed, I plan ahead to wake up half an hour earlier so I can fit in some me-time. What a great way to start the day! This me-time is not just about relaxation but about empowering oneself to handle life's stresses with resilience, whether at home or work.

Incorporating daily habits that foster a positive mindset became a part of my recovery. Movement, I found, was a powerful catalyst for change. A mere fifteen-minute walk each day would dramatically uplift my spirits, sparking those endorphins necessary for mental clarity and focus. This simple act of walking, especially when done without the distraction of electronics, allowed me to immerse myself in the present and appreciate the beauty around me while dismissing the negatives. Such small, consistent habits accumulated into significant progress.

You would be surprised how even a ten- or fifteen-minute walk can do your mind wonders. If you can, get out of the house or office to take your walk, preferably, as mentioned above, without any electronics stuck in your ear. Be in the moment of your walk, noticing your surroundings—be it nature or people. Notice the good—people smiling and being productive, birds singing, flowers—and not the bad—trash on the streets, cars honking, and so forth. Small habits done consistently stack up to big gains.

Inspired by the principles in the books *Atomic Habits* by

James Clear and *Tiny Habits* by B. J. Fogg, PhD, I began doing two push-ups at the sink after each bathroom break. Before I knew it, I was doing five floor push-ups, a small victory that propelled me to ask, *What else am I capable of?* I discovered that getting your body moving is one excellent way to trigger those endorphins to kick-start your mind to focus on the right track and not down the spiral staircase into the dark dungeon of your traumatic past. I have never been able to do any push-ups, but I started doing two push-ups at the sink each time I went to the bathroom, after washing my hands. The washing of my hands was the trigger I used to prompt me to do my push-ups right there at the sink. Nothing fancy, just do it. After only about a couple of weeks, I was able to do five actual push-ups on the floor. In no time, I was able to keep up with the rest of my Les Mills Bodypump class, doing all kinds of moves I had not been able to do before.

Try it. Once you have these small wins, you will be motivated to do more and will wake up one day and realize your thoughts are focused less and less on your painful past and more so on the joy you feel in seeing how far you have come!

I also keep a note on my phone and on a Post-it on my desk that helps remind me to be kind to myself because I am my harshest critic. I read this out loud to myself every day:

Treat myself well and kindly—no harsh judgment, forgive myself when I make mistakes, love myself—I am not broken and don't need to be fixed.

Here are some practical steps for implementing self-care:

- Schedule me-time: Just as I have, you can block out dedicated time daily for self-care activities that energize and center you. This might involve calls to a loved one or friend, hobbies, or simply quiet time away from the demands of daily life.

- Physical activity: Echoing the benefits of movement, I encourage incorporating simple physical activities like walking or yoga into daily routines. These activities not only improve physical health but also enhance mental clarity and emotional well-being.

- Mindfulness practices: Meditation, deep-breathing exercises, and journaling can profoundly impact one's ability to manage stress and maintain mental health. These practices help anchor the mind in the present moment, reducing anxiety and fostering a peaceful state of being.

- Connect with nature: Stepping outside, disconnecting from digital devices, and immersing oneself in nature can be incredibly therapeutic. Whether it's a short walk in a park or on a trail or spending time in a garden, nature has a way of healing and restoring our spirits.

Lay Out a Plan in Advance

Creating a productive plan to counter negative self-talk is essential for personal development.

Personal

I put together a plan for how I will react when negative thoughts about myself pop up—that is, the proverbial devil on my left shoulder telling me, "You are not good enough. You can't do it. Who will listen to you? You are ugly. Who do you think you are?" etc., etc. I use the word *cancel* forcefully, out loud. Each time, I shout "Cancel!" and sometimes add, "That's not true!" The first few times I did this, I felt utterly ridiculous, but I committed to doing it for a month, and I persisted. The more I did this, the better I felt because my negative thought patterns were interrupted.

Consider incorporating positive affirmations that reinforce your self-worth and capabilities. Each morning, or when negative thoughts arise, counter them with affirmations such as "I am capable and strong" or "I am worthy of respect and love." This not only negates the negative but also builds a positive framework in your mindset.

Professional

In the workplace, where it is not appropriate to shout out loud, I use my right hand to reach up to my left shoulder and forcefully brush off the imaginary devil standing there taunting me with those negative words. These actions very effectively break my negative thought process. Some time ago, I did this when I was in the office after I volunteered to do something for the team. That same devil popped up on my left shoulder and immediately shouted, "You stupid girl, why did you do that? You know you're super busy; you don't have the time and can't speak to more than two people without sweating it." He didn't even wait for me to get back to my office! With as much force as I could muster, I brushed him away and actually imagined him tumbling down off my shoulder, smacking the floor with a loud splat! The image made me giggle to myself, and that negative thought completely vanished! Try it; it works! Today, I don't sweat over conversing with a few people and am even comfortable speaking to a large audience.

Another way to visualize this is with a stop sign or a red light, which serves as a cue to halt the negative thought. Follow this up by mentally reviewing a list of your professional achievements or positive feedback received from colleagues, which can serve as a tangible reminder of your capabilities and value in your professional environment. Keeping a success journal at your desk where you record positive feedback, accomplishments, and moments of growth can be an effective way to combat workplace negativity and can be used as a go-to resource during moments of self-doubt, helping to shift your focus from self-criticism to self-appreciation.

None of these habits are things you do once or twice to smash those negative thoughts. The negative thoughts are going to come back again and again, so you will need to do these tricks every single time they surface. Remember, the key to success with this strategy is consistency. Make these practices a regular part of your daily routine to ensure they become second nature. Over time, you will find these negative thoughts diminish significantly in both frequency and impact. As time goes on, you can create different ways to topple this devil. I'm so good at this now that occasionally when he does appear on my shoulder, I'm so quick at knocking him off his feet that he doesn't even have a chance to open his big, filthy mouth. This puts a huge smile on my face, and I stride off confidently with my head held high and my chest out, feeling super strong. What a wonderful feeling to defeat this little devil!

Compartmentalize

In my quest for financial security and professional success, I discovered the indispensable strategy of compartmentalization. This approach was not imparted to me by anyone, rather, it evolved out of sheer necessity—a testament to human resilience and adaptability (necessity is the mother of invention). This strategy of compartmentalization has been a pivotal tool in my psychological toolbox I've used almost daily in managing the dual demands of my professional and personal life. By mentally segregating my work from my personal issues, I have been able to maintain focus and productivity in each sphere without the interference of the other.

Compartmentalizing, for me, meant creating a mental demarcation between my work life and personal affairs. If the night before was marred by turmoil, as it was many times, courtesy of my ex-husband, I would set a firm intention on my way to work: this can wait until I'm home. At work, I activated the same mental switch, allowing me to immerse fully in my professional responsibilities, untethered by personal distress. Initially, this required constantly reminding myself to stay focused on work, but with time, flipping this switch became second nature. This was my way to refocus and delay dealing with things outside of work that could wait.

This practice of compartmentalization was transformative. It allowed me to be fully present in the moment, whether I was navigating the demands of my job or cherishing time with my children at home. By dedicating specific times to process personal emotions, I could give my undivided attention to my work during the day or to my children in the evening, and then address my feelings of hurt or anger in the privacy of the night.

The Benefits and Drawbacks of this Strategy

Compartmentalization offered several benefits, notably improved focus, productivity at work, and enhanced emotional regulation. It served as a critical stress-management tool, helping me to maintain a clear boundary between professional duties and personal life challenges.

However, this strategy is not without its pitfalls. Overreliance on compartmentalization can lead to emotional detachment and avoidance. By continually boxing away emotions, there's a risk of becoming disconnected from one's feelings, potentially straining personal relationships and hindering emotional intimacy. Furthermore, using compartmentalization as a means to indefinitely delay dealing with personal issues can prevent the resolution of underlying problems, leading to accumulated emotional distress.

Compartmentalization is a double-edged sword. While it can be an effective short-term coping mechanism for managing stress and enhancing task performance, long-term reliance without addressing underlying emotional issues can contribute to emotional suppression and avoidance. Cognitive psychology suggests that compartmentalization can improve cognitive function by reducing overload but emphasizes the importance of balanced emotional processing.

Moving Forward with Balance

My journey with compartmentalization underscores the importance of using this strategy judiciously. It's crucial to strike a balance—leveraging the benefits of compartmentalization for focus and productivity while ensuring that it does not lead to avoidance or emotional disconnection. Regular self-reflection, emotional processing, and, when necessary, seeking professional guidance can help maintain this balance, allowing for both professional success and emotional well-being. I suffered too long by stuffing all my hurts deep inside and not taking enough time for myself to process the pain.

When first developing this skill, start small by identifying cues that will help you switch contexts, such as a specific playlist for work or a relaxing cup of tea in the evening. Over time, these cues can help solidify the mental habit of compartmentalizing, making the transition between personal and professional life smoother and more automatic. Once mastered, compartmentalization can significantly reduce stress and increase your ability to handle multiple aspects of life more effectively. It did for me.

Gratitude

Let me tell you about the power of gratitude—it can transform the mundane into the extraordinary, revealing the beauty and worth in what we might have previously overlooked. It's about acknowledging the good in our lives and understanding that, even in times of hardship, there are elements worthy of appreciation. This shift in perspective can significantly impact our mental health, reducing stress, fostering a sense of inner peace, and illuminating the richness of our lives. Here are some ways I've incorporated gratitude into my daily life that are applicable in both your personal and professional space:

- Keeping a journal: I end my day by writing down three things I'm grateful for. These can be as simple as there being no rain or snow that day, the comfort of a friend's support, or even the satisfaction of a well-made meal. Over time, this practice can help shift your focus from what is lacking to what is abundant in your life. Knowing that I am going to write down three things I am grateful for at the end of the day causes me to be on the lookout for things I can be grateful for. Super cool! What a way to live!
- To go deeper, try to find something to be grateful for in difficult situations. This might be learning from a mistake

you made at work, finding strength in adversity, or appreciating the opportunity for growth. Viewing challenges through the lens of gratitude can transform obstacles into opportunities.

- Expressing gratitude to others: I look for things I can thank people for, even small things they do, whether it's a colleague who helped me with a project or a loved one who listened to me after a hard day. Something my husband does when we go on road trips and stop at a rest area is that when he happens upon a janitor in the men's room, he often thanks them for keeping it clean. Without fail, every single time he's had an opportunity to do this, he sees the janitor's eyes light up and a big smile break out. Expressing gratitude not only uplifts the recipient but also reinforces your own feelings of thankfulness.

- Practicing mindful appreciation: I take moments throughout my day to pause and appreciate my surroundings. This could be while I am out and about running errands or taking a walk in the evening around my neighborhood or on a trail, consciously noticing the beauty of nature and finding joy in the simplicity of routine.

- Volunteering: Giving back to the community is a powerful way to cultivate gratitude. Employers often organize projects with charitable organizations like Habitat for Humanity or Feed My Hungry Children, and participating in them is a great way to work with colleagues in expressing our gratitude for what we have by giving back to society. On a personal level, we can volunteer our time at charitable organizations. I've volunteered my time at hospitals, doing minor tasks for patients; at juvenile detention centers, helping minors to read; and at food pantries, either at intake or stocking and serving customers. These opportunities helped me more than I helped others—they made me aware of how blessed I am that I have my health, my mind, and food on the table.

- Engaging in random acts of kindness: Engaging in random acts of kindness without expecting anything in return is one of my favorite things to do because it gives me such joy! The key words here are "without expecting anything in return." When doing so at work, people are oftentimes suspicious of your intentions at first. When they realize no ulterior or hidden motives are tied to these acts, special relationships are forged. On the personal side, it could be something as simple as complimenting a stranger, volunteering your skills, or paying for someone's coffee. The joy you will see on the recipient's face is just priceless. There is no room in our minds for any negative thoughts in those precious moments!

- Performing an annual gratitude review: Once a year, take time to review your gratitude journal or think back over the past year. Take the time to pause and reflect on the moments and people who are or even were significant to you. This annual practice can provide a deeper appreciation for the journey you've traveled and the growth you've experienced.

Research has shown that gratitude is linked to increased happiness, improved health, and stronger relationships. A study published in the *Journal of Personality and Social Psychology* found that individuals who regularly practice gratitude report fewer health problems and experience more optimism and happiness.[14]

While the practice of gratitude is profoundly beneficial, it can sometimes be challenging to maintain, especially during periods of intense stress or grief. It's important to acknowledge these feelings and understand that gratitude isn't about ignoring pain or difficulties but about finding a glimmer of light within them.

My suggestion would be to start small. Gratitude doesn't require grand gestures or monumental discoveries. It starts with noticing the little joys and comforts that fill your days. By integrating practices of gratitude into your life, you'll find that even in the darkest of times, there's always something to be thankful for. Remember, gratitude is like a muscle—the more you use it, the stronger it becomes.

Embracing gratitude is a journey, one that can profoundly change how you see the world and interact with it. Embrace gratitude as a lifestyle and let it be your guide, leading you to a life marked by joy, resilience, and an unshakable appreciation for the beauty that surrounds you.

Continuous Improvement

Continuous improvement is the practice of always seeking to be better, learn more, and refine our skills and knowledge. It is pivotal not just in overcoming adversity but in every aspect of life. It is about adopting a mindset that views every experience as an opportunity for growth and learning. This philosophy is critical for anyone coming from a place of trauma because it shifts the focus from surviving to thriving. In our journey through finding moments of joy amid adversity, embracing patience, taking baby steps toward a positive mindset, laying out a plan to counter negative thoughts, compartmentalizing, practicing gratitude, and now continuously improving, each step plays a crucial role in this holistic approach. Healing and personal growth are ongoing, marked by the understanding that there is always room for self-improvement. Continuous improvement, in the context of recovering from trauma and embracing life's joys, is about recognizing that our current selves are not our final selves. It's about seeking to learn, grow, and evolve beyond the person we are today. This concept, well encapsulated in author Marshall Goldsmith's *What Got You Here Won't Get You There*, serves as a reminder that the tools and behaviors that helped us survive may not be the ones that will help us thrive.[15]

We can start to integrate continuous improvements into our daily lives in four ways:

- Learning from feedback: Whether it's personal feedback from friends and family or professional feedback at work, embrace these insights as opportunities for growth. Reflect on the feedback, identify actionable points, and plan steps to implement improvements.
- Setting growth goals: Define clear, achievable goals related to both personal development and professional skills. These goals should push you slightly out of your comfort zone to encourage growth but remain realistic enough to keep you motivated.
- Regular self-assessment: Establish a routine self-assessment to evaluate your progress toward these goals. This could be through monthly reviews or by using tools like journals or apps designed to track personal growth.
- Continuous learning: Engage regularly in educational activities that enhance both your personal and professional knowledge. This could involve reading books,

attending workshops, or taking courses related to areas you're passionate about, such as emotional resilience, leadership, or a new hobby.

Particularly for those recovering from trauma, understanding the dynamics of abuse and violence can empower us to recognize unhealthy patterns and make informed decisions about our futures. Educating ourselves on these topics can help us recognize early warning signs and better manage future relationships as well.

Incorporating continuous improvement into our recovery strategies means setting personal and professional growth goals that challenge us to stretch beyond our comfort zones. It involves embracing feedback as a means of learning, cultivating a growth mindset that welcomes challenges as opportunities for development, and engaging in lifelong learning to adapt and respond to life's ever-changing landscape. Regular reflection on our growth journey helps us to recognize our progress and reassess our goals.

Look for the Gains, Not the Gaps

When I learned this powerful concept from Dr. Benjamin Hardy, it was transformative in bolstering my self-confidence and self-worth, and it altered the way I perceive my progress and achievements. Although I had had many successes, especially in my career, I had not been able to enjoy those successes because I focused on the "gaps" (what I did not achieve). Dr. Hardy emphasizes the common tendency to dwell on unmet goals or "gaps" in our accomplishments, which can overshadow the "gains" or successes we've achieved along the way. This focus on what's lacking, instead of on what's been accomplished, skews our perception of progress and can lead to feelings of inadequacy and stagnation.[16]

For instance, consider the goal of becoming more physically fit. You might set a target to run five miles without stopping, but after months of training, you can only run three miles. Focusing on the gap would mean fixating on the two miles you can't run, overlooking the progress you made from not running at all to completing three miles! The gain here is not just the physical ability to run three miles; it's also the discipline, persistence, and improvement in physical health that came with the training. Recognizing these gains shifts the narrative from one of failure to one of significant personal growth and achievement.

To incorporate this mindset into your life, start by reflecting on your recent endeavors or long-term goals. Instead of cataloging where you fell short, list out what you've accomplished, no matter how small those achievements may seem. This practice not only affirms your progress but also fosters a sense of gratitude and fulfillment that propels you forward. Journaling can also help here; when you look back in your journal, you can see your journey in making that progress, and that can be inspirational.

When I started to embrace this mindset of valuing gains over gaps, I felt profoundly liberated. I saw how many challenges I had overcome, both in my personal life and in my career, and I knew I could do the same with any other challenges that came my way. Believe me, they will come. That is why adopting a continuous improvement mindset will keep us alert and prepared for what is ahead. I always tell my children and teams at work that the day we think we know or have it all, we stop learning and improving. When we embrace a growth mindset, it encourages positive self-perception, fosters gratitude for the journey, and cultivates an environment where continuous growth is celebrated. Remember, every step forward, no matter its size, is a gain worth acknowledging and building upon.

By shifting our focus from what we've yet to achieve to what we've already accomplished, we not only boost our self-confidence but also redefine our path to success as one marked by continuous learning and appreciation for the journey. This mindset becomes a cornerstone for building a life filled with self-acceptance, achievement, and the joy of ongoing personal and professional development. This step is profound and can change the direction of your life and your career! It's a crucial mindset for anyone looking to foster self-acceptance, achieve meaningful goals, and enjoy the journey of personal and professional development.

Seek Professional Help

Seeking professional help, such as therapy and counseling, can be immensely beneficial for both healing from past traumas and learning to navigate current abusive relationships at work or home. Therapists can provide tools to help one cope, build self-esteem, and set boundaries.

- Finding the right therapist: Don't be discouraged if your first therapist doesn't work out. Keep doing your research either online or by asking friends for recommendations. It's essential to recognize that not every therapist will be the right fit. If the first one doesn't meet your needs, don't hesitate to seek another. This process is akin to finding the right medical doctor; personal comfort and professional expertise are key.

- Utilizing online resources: Make use of online directories and mental health platforms that offer therapist profiles, specialties, and patient reviews. These resources can help you find a therapist whose expertise aligns with your specific needs. Many companies offer mental health benefits; talk to your human resources or benefits department, who can confidentially connect you with the right therapist.
- Asking for recommendations: Don't overlook the power of personal recommendations. Ask friends, family, or even your general practitioner for referrals to therapists who have effectively helped others.

Let Go and Forgive

This final tool I have in my toolbox is the hardest for me.

First, it's important to understand that forgiving an abuser is not about absolving them of their actions or diminishing the severity of the harm they've caused. Rather, it's about the victim regaining power over their emotional well-being and releasing the hold that the painful experiences and the abuser have on their life.

Personal

For years, my perspective of my father was clouded by the memories of the pain he inflicted on my mom and the extreme fear I felt throughout my childhood. This narrative painted him in a light that allowed no room for redemption or understanding. However, as I matured, I grew to become a better version of myself. The more I delved into my quest for healing, the more I encountered a realization of something similar to the misconception harbored by Alan's family toward me. Their refusal to see beyond their belief that I was a gold digger and a "bitch" was a mirror reflecting my own inability to look past my father's abusive actions.

Forgiveness, especially in the context of domestic abuse, is a complex and deeply personal process. It's essential to recognize that forgiveness does not mean condoning or excusing abusive behaviors, nor does it require reconciliation with the abuser. Instead, forgiveness can be seen as a powerful step toward healing and liberation for the victim.

Below is a nuanced exploration of why victims, particularly of domestic abuse, might choose to forgive, the need for forgiveness, and the benefits it can bring.

Professional

On the professional level, if you feel someone has wronged you in the workplace, there are steps you can take:

- Reflect on the situation: Assess the incident from a neutral perspective to understand the context and motivations that may have led to the perceived wrong.
- Communicate openly: If possible, have a candid conversation with the person involved to express your feelings and hear their side of the story. This can clear up misunderstandings quickly.
- Empathize: Try to understand the situation from the other person's point of view. Acknowledging that everyone makes mistakes can make forgiveness easier.
- Let go of grudges: Holding onto resentment can be harmful to your own mental health and workplace harmony. Actively decide to let go of the grudge.
- Seek to rebuild trust gradually: Forgiveness doesn't mean you ignore the past, but it can be the first step toward

rebuilding trust. Start with small, low-risk projects to rebuild your professional relationship.

- Focus on the positive: Redirect your energy toward positive interactions and contributions at work. Recognize your colleagues' strengths and contributions to improve the work environment.
- Professional help: If workplace conflicts are severe, consider mediation or speaking to a human resources representative to facilitate the process.

Why Victims Might Choose to Forgive

- Emotional release: Holding onto anger and resentment can be emotionally draining and perpetuate the victim's suffering. Forgiveness allows for the release of these burdensome feelings, leading to emotional relief and peace.
- Healing and recovery: Forgiveness is often a critical step in the healing process. It enables the victim to move past the trauma, reducing feelings of bitterness and victimhood, and fostering resilience.
- Regaining control: By choosing to forgive, victims reclaim control over their emotional state. It's a proactive step toward not letting the abuser's actions define their self-worth or future happiness.
- Breaking the cycle: Forgiveness can help prevent the transference of anger and hurt to other relationships and aspects of life. It allows victims to respond to their current life and future relationships with a healthier, more positive outlook.

The Benefits of Forgiving

- Improved mental health: Forgiveness can lead to better mental health outcomes, such as reduced symptoms of anxiety, depression, and post-traumatic stress disorder.
- Enhanced self-esteem: Letting go of anger and resentment can boost self-esteem and self-worth, as the victim no longer identifies solely with their trauma.
- Better relationships: Forgiveness can improve the victim's ability to form and maintain healthy relationships in the future, based on trust and mutual respect rather than fear and suspicion.
- Spiritual growth: For some, like me, forgiveness is also a spiritual journey that aligns with their values and beliefs about compassion, love, and the possibility of redemption.

It's important to approach the subject of forgiveness with care, especially in the case of domestic abuse. While forgiveness can offer numerous benefits as outlined, it's important to emphasize a vital note of caution: *depending on each individual's circumstances, forgiveness may not be possible, advisable, or even safe.*

The safety and well-being of the victim should always be the paramount concern. In situations where forgiving an abuser might lead to further harm, endangerment, or even a potential reconciliation that could put the victim at risk, forgiveness may not be the appropriate path.

Forgiveness requires a significant amount of emotional work and healing. Victims should never feel pressured to forgive before they are ready. Doing so prematurely can hinder the healing process and potentially lead to further emotional distress. Forgiveness is just one aspect of healing. Some individuals may find that their path to healing does not include forgiveness, and that is entirely valid. The healing process is highly individualized, and what works for one person may not be suitable for another.

Forgiveness *does not* equate to either allowing the abuser back into one's life or lowering one's guard against potential harm. It's crucial to maintain strong boundaries to protect oneself and any loved ones. Forgiveness can be done in a psychological or emotional sense, and it does not necessitate contact with the abuser or any form of relationship. Healing can take many forms, and victims should feel empowered to explore various avenues of recovery that resonate with their needs and circumstances. Therapy, support groups, creative expression, and focusing on building a positive future are all valid and potentially healing alternatives.

Given the complexities surrounding forgiveness in the context of domestic abuse, seeking professional guidance from therapists or counselors who specialize in trauma and recovery can provide invaluable support. They can help navigate the emotional terrain of forgiveness, ensuring that any steps taken toward it are in the best interest of the victim's emotional and physical safety.

While forgiveness can be a powerful step toward healing and reclaiming one's life, it's not a journey that every victim can or should embark upon. It's essential to honor each individual's unique circumstances, emotional state, and safety needs. Forgiveness should never compromise a victim's well-being or safety, and there should be no judgment or pressure to forgive. Each person's path to healing is their own, and for some, it may not include forgiveness. The priority should always be the victim's health, safety, and personal growth, whether that includes forgiveness or not.

If you're in an abusive relationship, here are a couple of additional steps you can take:

- Safety planning: Having a safety plan in place is essential. Should you deem it is time to leave your situation, reach out to domestic violence hotlines or shelters for guidance on how to safely leave an abusive situation.
- Legal and community support: Explore legal options for protection, such as restraining orders. Local community organizations and support groups can offer resources and assistance.

Embrace Your Journey: Unleash Your Iron Will

My dear readers, as we part ways, through the pages of this journey, I leave you with a whisper of truth to carry in your heart . . . You possess a resilience and strength far greater than you've ever imagined. In moments of shadow, when clarity seems just beyond reach, hold tightly to the faith that guides you—faith in the unwavering belief that, beyond the storms, there is light. Remember, the darkest nights often lead to the brightest mornings. May this faith be the beacon that leads you through uncertainty, the anchor in your moments of doubt, and the wind that propels you forward when the path ahead clears.

With all my heart, I wish you the very best. Embrace your journey with courage, for within you lies an invincible spirit capable of overcoming any challenge—your iron will!

I can do
all things
through Him who
STRENGTHENS
PHILIPPIANS 4:13 ME.

YOUR JOURNEY TO EMPOWERMENT AND RESILIENCE DOESN'T END HERE!

To help you implement the strategies found inside this book and measure your progress, I am excited to offer you a **FREE** workbook and self-assessment test!

What you will get:

- A workbook with practical exercises, reflection questions, and actions steps to help you apply the powerful concepts you read about in *Iron Will* to your daily life.
- A self-assessment test to help you gauge your emotional and professional resilience. This test can be taken as often as you would like.

Sign up to receive your free workbook and self-assessment test at:
www.wendycwilson.com/iron-will

I recommend taking the self-assessment test as a first step before diving into the workbook. Then, continue to take the test at intervals both during and after you've completed the workbook to see and track your improvements over time.

By taking this next step, you are committing to your personal and professional growth. I am thrilled to accompany you on this journey and can't wait to see the incredible progress I know you'll make!

With gratitude,
Wendy C. Wilson

Acknowledgments

AT THE HEART OF THIS BOOK lies the gratitude I owe to those who have been the architects of my journey toward a better self.

To my husband, Alan. Your unwavering belief in me and your endless support have been the cornerstones of this journey. Your encouragement and love not only fuel my dreams but also transform them into reality. Every word on these pages has been inspired by the strength you give me daily, and for that, I am eternally grateful.

To my children, Samantha and Adrian. You are my North Stars, guiding me through the darkest nights and keeping me on my path toward my true purpose. Your laughter, curiosity, and zest for life remind me every day that there is beauty in the world and of the endless possibilities that lie ahead. You remind me of who I am, who I strive to be, and the reasons I have to forge ahead.

To all three of you, my deepest thanks for your unwavering support, love, and belief in me. This journey would not have been possible without you by my side. This book is a testament to the strength you've given me.

To my hero Ed Mylett, whose wisdom and strength have been a beacon of inspiration—I wrote this book because you told me my pain "qualifies me" to do so. To my mentors and coaches: Brendon Burchard for your invaluable guidance in teaching me how to keep growing to become a better version of myself and to be courageous in taking the steps necessary to go after my dreams. To Jamie Kern Lima, who taught me how to fight the demons who told me I was not worthy. And to Sheena, Ashley, and all my Ultra friends, whose encouragement and unwavering support have bolstered my resolve.

Special acknowledgment and gratitude goes to Ashley Mansour and her dedicated team, whose expertise not only shaped my thoughts into words but brought this narrative to life.

Your collective belief in my story has been the cornerstone of this endeavor. Thank you for being the pillars that uphold my dreams.

WENDY C. WILSON spent a distinguished thirty-five-year career in corporate America before retiring. Early in her career, she served for over two years as a CFO at a benefits consulting firm, and later became a leader for global procurement and supplier management teams.

Throughout her life, Wendy has faced and overcome numerous challenges, childhood traumas, an abusive seven-year marriage, and workplace bullying and discrimination. After retiring, she reflected deeply on these harrowing experiences and came to realize they taught her invaluable lessons about resilience, grit, and the power of a focused mindset—lessons she now aims to share with the world through her stories.

To learn more about Wendy, visit *www.wendycwilson.com*

Check out her blog at *www.wendycwilson.com/blog*, where she shares strategies and tips on how to successfully navigate and resolve corporate challenges faced by many in the workplace.

For all media inquiries or other questions,
reach out to *hello@wendycwilson.com*

Endnotes

1   Prov. 13:24 (NIV).

2   LeWine, Howard E. "Understanding the Stress Response." Harvard Health. June 15, 2011. *https://www.health.harvard.edu/ staying-healthy/understanding-the-stress-response.*

3   Lewine, "Understanding the Stress Response."

4   Lupien, Sonia, Bruce McEwen, Megan Gunnar, and Chrstine Heim. "Effects of Stress throughout the Lifespan on the Brain, Behaviour and Cognition." Nature Reviews Neuroscience 10 (May 1, 2009): 434–45. *https://doi.org/10.1038/nrn2639.*

5   Steptoe, Andrew, and Mika Kivimäki. "Stress and Cardiovascular Disease: An Update on Current Knowledge." Annual Review of Public Health 34 (March 18, 2013): 337–54. *https://doi.org/10.1146/ annurev-publhealth-031912-114452.*

6   Haykin, Hedva, and Asya Rolls. "The Neuroimmune Response during Stress: A Physiological Perspective." Immunity 54, no. 9 (September 14, 2021): 1933–47. *https://doi.org/10.1016/j. immuni.2021.08.023.*

7   Sinha, Rajita. "Chronic Stress, Drug Use, and Vulnerability to Addiction." Annals of the New York Academy of Sciences 1141, no. 1 (2008): 105–30. *https://doi.org/10.1196/annals.1441.030.*

8   McKinsey & Co. and LeanIn.Org. "Women in the Workplace." Lean In. Accessed May 28, 2024. *https://leanin.org/ women-in-the-workplace/2020/the-state-of-the-pipeline*.

9   Subhani, Ovais. "Economists Raise Singapore's 2024 Growth Forecast on Hopes of Global Demand Pickup: MAS Survey." The Straits Times. March 13, 2024. *https://www.straitstimes.com/ business/economists-raise-singapore-s-2024-growth-forecast-on-hopes-of-global-demand-pickup-mas-survey*.

10   Credit Suisse AG. "Global Wealth Report 2023." UBS Family Office & UHNW. Accessed May 28, 2024. *https://www.ubs.com/ global/en/family-office-uhnw/reports/global-wealth-report-2023. html*.

11   Ziglar Inc. "Home Page." Accessed May 29, 2024. *https://www. ziglar.com/home-page-new/*.

12   Goodreads. "Whether You Think You Can, or You Think You Can't—You're Right." Accessed May 29, 2024. *https://www.go-odreads.com/quotes/978-whether-you-think-you-can-or-you-think-you-can-t--you-re*.

13   Phil. 4:13 (NKJV).

14   Gordon, Amie M., Emily A. Impett, Aleksandr Kogan, Christopher Oveis, and Dacher Keltner. "To Have and to Hold: Gratitude Promotes Relationship Maintenance in Intimate Bonds." Journal of Personality and Social Psychology 103, no. 2 (August 2012): 257–74. *https://doi.org/10.1037/a0028723*.

15   Goldsmith, Marshall, and Mark Reiter. "What Got You Here Won't Get You There: How Successful People Become Even More Successful". Hyperion, 2007.

16   Sullivan, Dan, and Benjamin Hardy. "The Gap and the Gain: The High Achievers' Guide to Happiness, Confidence, and Success". Hay House, Inc, 2021.